Wild Word

WILD WORDS

Rituals, Routines, and Rhythms for Braving the Writer's Path

Nicole Gulotta

Roost Books
Boulder

Roost Books
An imprint of Shambhala Publications, Inc.
4720 Walnut Street
Boulder, Colorado 80301
roostbooks.com

"Morning" by Mary Oliver from *New and Selected Poems, Vol. 1* by Mary Oliver.
Published by Beacon Press, Boston. © 1992 by Mary Oliver. Reprinted by
permission of The Charlotte Sheedy Literary Agency Inc.
"Air" by W. S. Merwin © 2017 by W. S. Merwin. Reprinted by permission of
the Wylie Agency LLC and Bloodaxe Books.

9 8 7 6 5 4 3 2 1

First Edition
Printed in the United States of America

⊛This edition is printed on acid-free paper that meets the
American National Standards Institute Z39.48 Standard.
♻ This book is printed on 30% postconsumer recycled paper.
For more information please visit www.shambhala.com.
Roost Books is distributed worldwide by
Penguin Random House, Inc., and its subsidiaries.

Library of Congress Cataloging-in-Publication Data
Names: Gulotta, Nicole, author.
Title: Wild words: rituals, routines, and rhythms for braving the writer's path / Nicole Gulotta.
Description: Boulder: Roost Books, 2019. | Includes bibliographical references and index.
Identifiers: LCCN 2018057640 | ISBN 9781611806656 (paperback)
Subjects: LCSH: Authorship. | Creative ability. | BISAC: REFERENCE / Writing Skills. |
SELF-HELP / Creativity. | SELF-HELP / Motivational & Inspirational.
Classification: LCC PN145 G7789 2019 | DDC 808.02—dc23
LC record available at https://lccn.loc.gov/2018057640

*If you've ever felt like
your voice wasn't enough,
this book is for you.*

Morning

Mary Oliver

Salt shining behind its glass cylinder.

Milk in a blue bowl. The yellow linoleum.

The cat stretching her black body from the pillow.

The way she makes her curvaceous response to the small, kind gesture.

Then laps the bowl clean.

Then wants to go out into the world

where she leaps lightly and for no apparent reason across the lawn,

then sits, perfectly still, in the grass.

I watch her a little while, thinking:

what more could I do with wild words?

I stand in the cold kitchen, bowing down to her.

I stand in the cold kitchen, everything wonderful around me.

Contents

Wild Words

Introduction

A Writer's Life Is Lived in Seasons

I.

The seed for this book was planted a few months after my son Henry was born, as he slept in a rocker next to our sectional. My husband left for work and I was hungry, so I crept into the kitchen to unwrap half a loaf of pumpkin bread and cut off a large slab. I cradled it under a folded paper towel and set it down on my desk, pulling off a moist corner to chew while I checked my email. The poem "Morning" by Mary Oliver caught my eye inside a daily poetry newsletter.

How beautifully she traced the simplicity of walking through the house as a fresh day dawned. A cat stretched, drank milk from a blue bowl. Nestled toward the end of the poem, a question beckoned: "What more could I do with wild words?" In that moment I felt it mine to answer, though I wasn't sure how.

I'd been rocking and nursing and swaddling my way through the early months with a newborn, where moments to myself were scarce. My baby seemed to know precisely the second I sat down with a cup of hot tea and would wake with cries, needing something from me. Finishing that cup, on rare occasions, was a triumph. But sleep-deprived as I was, I still felt the deep contentment Oliver spoke of. "Everything wonderful around me," she wrote.

Everything was, in fact, quite wonderful. I was happy and grateful to be on the other side of pregnancy with a darling boy in my arms. I looked around the room. Bottles dried in their special rack meant to look like grass, next to the sink. A sliver of light beamed through our large kitchen window, revealing shimmering flecks of dust on the countertop. A plate sat nearby holding a few crumbs from my first slice of pumpkin bread earlier that morning, before the sun rose.

The poem is about paying attention to your life. It's the writer's work—our privileged work—to observe, to notice, to record. After all, ordinary moments are often where we find the deepest meaning. The phrase *wild words* rose up from the page and I stored it in my heart, but it would be years before this book would grow from seed to sprout.

I'd only recently finished the manuscript for my first book, *Eat This Poem: A Literary Feast of Recipes Inspired by Poetry*, and my maternity leave was the window of opportunity to corral recipe testers and work on copy edits. Three months later, after color-coding spreadsheets and baking coffee cake for the fifth time, I hit *send* on an email with a large attachment called "ETP MANUSCRIPT—FINAL." I'd written a book, something I'd always wanted to do, but I'll say this now: I was deeply afraid I'd never be able to do it again. How could I write another book when I could barely manage to blow-dry my hair and I lived my days in three-hour increments, moving from one feeding to the next? Life had changed irrevocably, and I wanted to know how writing would survive all this—changing diapers, reading parenting books, ordering baby shampoo, recording bowel movements into an app on my phone. It went on and on.

Although my hours are no longer measured by feedings, the fear of writing slipping away is somehow still visceral. Not constant, but present, more like a shadow. As content as I feel with family life, my creativity has been constricted like organs during pregnancy, collapsed onto one another in perpetual discomfort. But because I'm a writer who still wants to write, I must move one day at a time, one word at a time, if necessary. There's no choice but to admit I know almost nothing, and begin again. Writing compels us to continue on no matter the circumstances, and although change may be uncomfortable, it's reliable. As life's transitions unfold—a move, a new job, a new partner, another child, the loss of loved ones—one way to weather the ups and downs is by establishing a new relationship with our creativity. Our writing can support us at every turn.

II.

Years ago, before I became a mother, a coworker told me something I've never forgotten: "A woman's life is lived in seasons." It felt like a secret passed from one friend to the next, like the telephone game we played as children, offering a profound piece of wisdom to help mark our days. I wrote the line in my journal and then, in the thick of the fourth trimester, probably while I was nursing and figuring out how to turn Kindle pages with my opposite hand, it occurred to me: a writer's life is lived in seasons too.

This truth grounds me and provides hope, especially when I'm desperate to write but am exhausted after getting home from work. On evenings like this I might have only half an hour to myself once the dinner, bath, and bed routine ends (The Season of Raising Young Children) or, when I was commuting, I may have lost two hours of a day on the road (The Season of Discontent).

My writing life faced frustrations before I had a baby, but in hindsight they were more manageable. I wasn't so tired, for one. And even with a full-time job, I had an enormous amount of free time at my disposal. Now Henry has just turned two, and as I settle into new ways of living and writing, I'm convinced embracing a seasonal approach to your creativity can change everything, because it roots you to your own innate rhythms in a way our social media–fueled, busy-as-a-badge-of-honor culture does not. This approach allows you the spaciousness to be exceedingly gracious with yourself, which happens to be good advice for both parenting and writing.

When the planet shifts from summer to fall, we feel it on our skin, see it in our gardens, eat its bounty at our tables. A certain sense of ease comes from welcoming these periods and knowing unequivocally where we're headed month after month. I find nurturing a sustainable writing practice is a gentler way to honor the years of work it takes to create almost anything worthwhile. Although it doesn't always eliminate moments of doubt, days of distractions, or challenges brought on by unforeseen causes, it does give our experiences a name. We can point to it. *There, I see you,* we say. Let's work through this together.

III.

When I think of wildness, I imagine elemental things—orange poppies springing up on hillsides, expansive coastlines with curling waves, heat rising from the asphalt of an open stretch of highway. Sometimes that kind of wildness feels other, like I'm near it but not of it. But there's also the wildness within us that lives among the daily comings and goings of shopping for groceries, filling the car with gas, taking children to the dentist: words, yearnings, and questions that stir in the writer's heart.

Finally, we have our bodies, which are vessels for creation. Every month a woman's cycle traces the four seasons in the deepest corners of her womb. We are winter: dark and cocooned, journaling and reading, keeping ourselves warm. We are spring: budding and new, tending soil, turning pages in fresh notebooks. We are summer: warm and bursting, picking tomatoes off the vine, creating every day. We are autumn: windy and whispering, harvesting ideas, finishing what we start.

Brené Brown calls the wilderness an "untamed, unpredictable place of solitude and searching. It is a place as dangerous as it is breathtaking." This must be the place our truth is unleashed. Most days are filled with the juxtaposition of going about our daily lives—how ordinary it all seems—with listening for the voice inside to offer the next sentence, the next idea. One way I've managed to access any wild words sitting right below the surface of my skin is to practice, as the psychologist Marion Woodman instructs, "holding the tension of the opposites" and finding a way through it, one season at a time.

The lessons you'll find on the coming pages are offered from someone who has been there, and is still there. A while back I developed a process that allowed me to write my first book while also working full time. As I started writing my second book, which you're reading, the reality of my life had shifted so dramatically I wasn't sure I could do it again. Temporarily, desire outweighed fear, so I decided to try, be flexible, and be instructed all over again.

And then the seasons emerged. Their framework allowed me to access writing in fresh ways—always meeting me where I was. I've lived and relived many of these seasons in the course of writing. The Season of Self-Doubt began shortly after penning my first words. There was The Season of Retreating, when I attended a workshop and wrestled with one of my deepest writing fears. All the while I've operated from The Season of Raising Young Children, negotiating between my day job and home life to mold uninterrupted time to write. I thought I was writing The Season of Discontent from a place of reflection, sharing something I went through a few years earlier, only to discover I'm here again. Except this time, I know how to get myself out of it. I'm sure you've moved through life this way too: felt changes take hold in your body and mind, struggled against what you can control and what you cannot. Take heart, you and I are not the first to struggle with this vocation.

Things are beginning to smooth over now. I have a rhythm. I have a few margins each week I can count on to write, but this is only because time has passed gently over, revealing with unmistakable clarity what my soul truly craved and teaching me to limit the distractions that set me off course. Having a baby helps put things into perspective, but it's not a requirement. What I'm here to tell you is that if you wish to write, you can. (Most likely, you must.) The work will probably take longer than you want it to. You'll be forced to make decisions about how to spend your time. You'll have fewer opportunities to binge-watch Netflix shows, for one. But there's room in this world for your stories, and we need them. You don't have to keep your voice hidden. You don't have to separate all the versions of yourself or reconcile your creative impulses with your desire to show up for other joys and responsibilities that bring meaning to your life. Seeking balance—which feels like we're teetering on the edge, straining to ready ourselves—is not the goal. Instead, let's resolve to blend. Writing, family, and work aren't isolated elements but moving parts with constant overlap that can inform, support, and even enhance one another.

When I first read Oliver's poem, I was in The Season of Liminal Space, the time between what was and what's to come, but I didn't know to call it that. Henry had just been born, and we were acclimating to life as a family of three as a deadline for my manuscript loomed. Her words spoke of everything beautiful about the writer's life, this journey I'm on and will always be on.

It reminded me that while I'd be temporarily *not* creating, the words would stay buried deep in the soil, waiting for spring. Your own wild words are there too, I know it.

Although I'm wary of making promises—mostly because I believe there are no secret formulas to follow except the wisdom of your own intuition—I vow to reveal with honesty and vulnerability the systems that have worked for me, the circumstances that challenged me, and the mind-set shifts I've made in order to see my life more clearly.

A note before we begin: Throughout this book, there are places to pause. When you're ready to implement some of the suggestions offered, you'll find them broken out into Rituals and Routines—markers to support your current season or connect more deeply with yourself, and activities to anchor to your writing life. As for rhythms, they're your own personal beat, like stirring cream into morning coffee or the way you hold your pen and move it across the page. Rhythms simply emerge from moving through your day. Along the way, I'll be your gentle guide as you embrace the season you're in. The only thing I ask is that you be open and curious. If you can do this, then I invite you to turn the page.

-1-

The Season of
Beginnings

*At the start of every new writing project, ideas
are planted in dark, nourishing soil. When energy
abounds, we embody messy first drafts, delight in fresh
sentences, and learn to write in the margins.*

You're not sure of the path. You're not even sure
where the next step will take you. When you
begin, whisper to yourself: *I don't know.*
—DANI SHAPIRO

Plucking Weeds

During a strange winter heat last March, I stood among kale leaves and pea shoots with a group of volunteers, thinking I should have brought a hat yet feeling grateful to be there at all after losing my GPS signal winding through Glassell Park's narrow roads. The thrill of trusting my own sense of north and south was as brief as the morning's cloud cover, but my memory of the map proved enough as I curved slowly down a long driveway until the plot came into view. Deep in the canyon, an oasis. Houses were tucked around the garden and knobby trees circled the perimeter, encasing rows of sunlit vegetables.

We were told a stretch of soil needed turning. I started with a hoe, using the ball of my foot and some strength in my shoulders to sink the hard metal blade into the ground. I agitated dirt all morning, stripping it of the season's bounty, squashes and onions no doubt. All around me, signs of spring, and just when I began to notice how thirsty I was, the weeds whispered.

As I walked to the edge of the garden and crouched into one of the few patches of shade, the woman in charge followed me and divulged that weeding is one of her favorite things to do, like a moving meditation. We met a couple of years ago, when I interviewed her for a magazine article. That's when I first learned of her efforts to establish wellness curriculums in local schools, which is where much of this produce is destined for.

Indeed, sitting in the grass, plucking and pulling, I was entranced. I watched the others haul away wheelbarrows full of cabbages larger than my head. The day's rhythm could be measured by the flick of a wrist. Pluck, pluck, pluck. Breathing slowed, the mind opened. The fertile basin seemed to murmur: *Nothing else matters. Be here now. Tend the soil. Pluck, pluck, pluck.*

Every plant begins as a seed. And inside a seed? The smallest speck of life—a root, a stem, a shoot, a cradle for food. Before the first word is written, our story remains buried alongside memories, hopes, questions, and cold mugs of tea, waiting in the dark. Under the right conditions, with proper care, might the ideas flourish? And after they've ascended from the dirt, might we have the patience and courage to work under the bright sun and muddy our hands beside long rows of sentences, pulling away everything that's unnecessary? To erase whole paragraphs that take readers nowhere, and to watch as those writing weeds pile up all around us? Whenever we begin, we tend the garden of our mind and help a story grow. This is our difficult and wonderful task.

Like me, you may have unfinished notebooks stacked on your bedside and in your purse, or documents saved on your computer storing half-written poems, lists of first lines, story ideas, names of characters. But life often reminds us that in the interest of time, we can't possibly care for every idea that's planted.

Some activities are perennials and can thrive year-round, such as journaling regularly or reading poetry daily. Annuals are scattered in the spring—add the right amount of water and reap the rewards come summer and fall. One year it might be the second draft of a novel, or a finished book proposal. So if you have only a handful of minutes, not hours, to dedicate, what should you write? One must be discerning. Facing this choice, I often ask myself, *What story do I need to tell right now?*

I should be honest, I almost didn't take my own advice. This book, in fact, was not the one I thought would come next, because I began by asking the wrong question: How can I write about the writer's life when my structured days feel suffocating and I write on my phone in ten-minute increments? But it's precisely because I'm still in new motherhood's messy depths, sometimes writing nothing for weeks and always lamenting how little time I have for *anything* (writing chief among this list of pleasures), that I must forge ahead and welcome you alongside me from beginning to end.

-Rituals & Routines-

PLANT YOUR STORY

What story do you need to tell right now? L. L. Barkat calls the stories that are ready today "now-stories." The other stories, and of course there are many, will ripen until they're ready to be twisted off stems like peaches from a tree in August.

Write down your ideas and look at them laid out, truly see them gazing back at you. Draw circles around some, cross out others, underline a few. These inklings are with you for a reason; it's merely a matter of which one speaks the loudest at this moment in time, and which one you're eager to explore for the next year or two, maybe longer. Which idea, if nurtured, will help you grow too? If you think too much about obstacles, you'll talk yourself out of writing, but if you observe what your soul has to say, you'll move forward, which is the only direction you need to go.

Writing in the Margins

Opening a fresh notebook and smoothing down the first page always sends a tingle up my spine. Those new, pure words formed in the womb of possibility are not yet weighed down by the challenge of finding time to complete whatever story was so optimistically started. Unfortunately, optimism fades and is replaced by the reality of this season: to become both flexible yet deliberate. You must hold opposing energies in your hands and create space for words to flow as they will. This requires being in tune with your rhythms and changing them, however often you need, until you feel supported, able to seize any opportunity, even if it's only a few minutes. I call this writing in the margins, and it's the one thing that's helped me write consistently, as one needs to do.

You might already be writing this way, without the name, but I like the formality because on days when I become distracted with other obligations (which is often), or feel like I've taken two steps back (also often), I remember how writing in the margins has anchored me for years now, and how three sentences will eventually become three paragraphs. How long does it take for a seed to sprout? How long does it take to write a first draft? It all depends on the plant and how it's nurtured.

Occasionally you can find me wandering through nurseries,

eager to bring a few colorful blooms home for the patio. Despite my enthusiasm, some flowers blossom while others, like my herb garden, wither. But the exercise teaches me something about writing. The flowers that thrive are given small amounts of care, daily or weekly as required. Sunday is my watering day. I walk through the house collecting every ceramic vase and pot, arranging them in the sink. Each mound of dirt gets a fresh spray of cold water, and I watch it pool on the surface before sinking beneath the rocks, reviving every root. I try to remember to approach my writing this way, and continue to believe one sentence at a time is enough. Sometimes it's all I can accomplish in a day, but you can write a whole book that way. I've only just begun.

-*Rituals & Routines*-
FIND YOUR MARGINS

This approach takes advantage of brief windows of time we have to spare. Writing in the margins is also the answer to the question I'm often asked: How do you do it? I always say, a little adds up to a lot; you can write a book in ten minutes a day. Keep trying new things until you discover what works.

Focus on what life looks like right now, this month, today. Inevitably, if you try this exercise a year from now, opportunities might be different. There's little to gain from dreaming up a perfect writing day only to find yourself squarely in the midst of an imperfect writing day. So before doing anything else, open up to the possibility of making space in your life just as it is.

Writing in the margins might be one of the ultimate rhythms to the writer's life, and in the best moments you'll feel as though you're doing it well and making inroads, that you're trusting the process and working with your creativity to unfurl. There are a few ways to find your margins.

First, your schedule. Address your weekdays and weekends separately, and start by writing down the obvious: The time you arrive to work, a lunch break, when you pick up a child or two from school, dinner, and so on. Open your calendar and ask yourself, *Is my schedule predictable, with standing meetings week to week, or is it often a surprise?* What's your routine immediately after waking up or returning home from work? Do you meet friends or coworkers for lunch, dinner, or happy hour? Do you watch television? Do you exercise? What has to stay, and what can you give up or modify? These are questions you may need to sit with and feel your way through.

Next, ponder spaces. Do you have a private office at work, a nearby park, or shared outdoor area? At home, where is your desk? Do you have one? Can you write in the car while you wait for appointments to start or dance classes to end?

With a few ideas brewing, you can experiment. As I'm sure you've gathered, there's no one way to write in the margins. Your ideal writing time could be at 1:35 p.m. when your youngest daughter takes a Saturday afternoon nap. Or writing may fall at 5:30 p.m. after you've arrived home from work and you have approximately twenty minutes before you hear the garage door open and your spouse and kids walk through the door. Time is necessary if you want to write, so searching for these margins is paramount.

If something changes—projects pick up at work, school's out for the summer, or you simply need time away to take care of yourself—always modify without hesitation. Throw out expectations and do what feels right in the moment or in a particularly challenging week. Seize opportunities to write, even in strange places and for the briefest of moments. One afternoon I was baking brownies and had to put the pan back in the oven for three more minutes so the center would set. I returned to my computer and wrote until the timer went off.

One Step Forward, Two Steps Back

It's Sunday afternoon, and my husband, Andrew, is working overtime to finish a project when the phone rings. His mother was just rushed to the emergency room. We scramble to make a plan and decide he'll skip work tomorrow and drive up to see his mom, returning Tuesday night. I can manage for thirty-six hours, I think.

Then Henry wakes with a high fever a little after midnight. We bathe him in lukewarm water and sing songs on the cool tiled floor, plus one more encore of *Twinkle, Twinkle, Little Star* before tucking him back into bed. I sleep terribly. In the morning, Andrew packs a duffel bag with a change of shirt and his toothbrush, and my body is giving me signs: it hurts to swallow. After breakfast I stumble into the kitchen to scrub the dishes that have been soaking. I eat a spoonful of local honey. I change my clothes, wash my face, rest on the bed, and reach for my phone to write all this down while Henry naps (one of my most predictable margins). I will forget otherwise.

By Tuesday morning I send Henry back to school and shuffle through the day. From my eyelids to my heart, everything is heavy, and as soon as Henry and I get home, the night routine starts. I make us plates of rigatoni with defrosted tomato sauce and rush through his bath, anticipating our ritual of saying "goodnight, sleep tight, I'll see you in the morning" before closing the bedroom door. Except he doesn't want to help put his toys away. He yells, cries, flails around the room and into a pile of pillows in the corner. I ask him to pick the two books we'll read together, but he refuses. It's time for bed, I say. Let's get into your crib.

Then rage rises from my stomach to the front of my forehead like flood water. Suddenly I'm not myself, a fact I know but cannot stop. I say no, we won't be reading any books tonight because you spent too much time telling me you didn't want to put your blocks away, snatch *Brown Bear, Brown Bear* from his hand, and toss it onto the shelf. There are more tears, and I wipe his nose and rub his back. Then we hold hands in the dark as I lay next to his crib. I tell him I know it's hard to have big feelings, and I know it's disappointing not to get things we want, but we can start fresh tomorrow. I apologize. "Do you want to start fresh with me?" I ask, and in his quietest whisper, "Yeah," he says. I kiss his soft forehead and pull a piece of his blonde hair between my thumb and index finger. "Goodnight, sleep tight, I'll see you in the morning."

Now I'm a little bit hungry, craving popcorn, but too tired to spend more time in the kitchen. I have lost all gentleness. It's already been a week since I touched my manuscript, and two if you count this week, which I assume will be lost as well. Google Docs remain open in browser tabs I refuse to close. Am I writing a book? Today, no. Today I am simply moving from morning to night, trying to fend off a cold. I'd hoped to finish my first draft by the month's end but am forced to keep my notes, unfinished thoughts, and odd autocorrects to be sorted through another day, which will be the day I calmly, intentionally begin again. Tomorrow, perhaps.

-Rituals & Routines-

FIVE WAYS TO BEGIN

I've noticed a pattern. Right before I'm about to give up, moments of clarity present themselves. It's a cruel but reliable truth. After finishing a draft of the proposal, I should be pleased with myself. Instead I harp on all there is still left to do: notes to organize, a table of contents to spruce up, a title and subtitle to brainstorm, sample chapters to draft. *What are you, little book?* I ask. I need you to speak.

For two weeks I do nothing but think—while driving, before falling asleep, during walks on my lunch break. Slowly, ideas surface. I write them all down, exhilarated but not yet clear on how to enter the story. One afternoon I return to Mary Oliver's poem and circle back to the tender scene. I feel like the woman in the poem, so I start to write about her and this new version of myself I'm working to understand. My body softens as I type because I know I've done it now. I've started. I've found a way in. Weeds will be plucked eventually, I'm certain of that, but today is for digging shallow holes, tucking in seeds, and covering them with a mound of moist soil. We write, we dig, we wait, we go on this way indefinitely.

I was offered this exercise at a writing retreat, and it can be used for anything—a paragraph, a poem, a short story—and especially if you're feeling like things aren't quite right but you're unsure what to change.

1. Set your timer for five minutes.
2. Write five new ways to start the piece.

I made the mistake of assuming this sounded too simple, but it's shockingly effective. Don't think, just start writing and stop when you have five new beginnings. When you've finished, go back and see which entry point feels most compelling and continue on from there. I've done this many times now, even for certain sections of this book. It's a truly wonderful prompt. Here's an example that I've written.

MUSINGS FOR THE NEW YEAR

1 I used to be the list maker and an enthusiastic creator of checkboxes. Every New Year's Eve I wrote at least ten goals to accomplish before the following December. There was comfort in the ritual, but I noticed many of the same goals—exercise more, write more, cook more—moved with me from one year to the next. So I shifted my approach, focusing less on the precise details of what I hoped to achieve externally and more on the inner work. I started asking myself what I needed more of.

2 A list of previous words:

Purpose

Open

Connect

Expand

3 A few months ago I read a travel essay about the Hoh Rain Forest in Washington State. I was riveted, the beauty of the place felt magnetic—moss-covered trees, the vastness. I left the article open on my computer until I finally realized why it struck me the way it did. I needed space. Physical, mental, all of it.

4 My word for the year is *space*.

5 Lines from my journal: The beauty of a word is you don't know everything at the start. It forms to you over the course of a year and becomes something entirely new. A word is just the beginning of something, embodying pure potential.

A Mistake to Avoid

I arrive at the museum fifteen minutes before it opens and descend into the parking garage. Backing into a spot, I'm prepared for an easy exit and send Andrew a quick text announcing my arrival. We'd arranged this a month ago, after coming for a family picnic. Pushing the stroller, I said how much I loved museums, almost sighing, and Andrew turned to me and suggested I come back here to write. He'd play with Henry for a few hours so I could walk around and get inspired. When we got home, I made a calendar invite on my phone and sent it to him.

In the corner of my eye I notice a white truck moving toward me, but I keep typing. "Hey!" a muffled voice yells. "Hey, ma'am?" I roll down my window halfway. "Did you see the sign?" he asks. "Have to flip the car around so you don't break your back window on the ledge there." "Oh sure, of course. Didn't even notice. Thanks," I fumble. He drives away before I rebuckle my seatbelt to reposition the car, but already my heart's thumping and I have to tell myself to take five deep breaths and forget about the incident all together. So the morning I set aside to start editing an early draft has begun by my failing to do the very thing a writer is supposed to do: pay attention.

After a slow tram ride to the hilltop, I settle in at a circular table next to a long pool with fountains dancing over the water. The rush of white noise drowns out any conversation as visitors pass on their way to the galleries, and I reach into my purse for a purple pen along with three printed chapters. When I took the pages off the printer this morning, I brought the stack to my nose and inhaled the warm smell of laser ink. It's like pulling a tin of cardamom muffins from the oven, marveling at their perfectly brown tops before biting in and scattering crumbs on your lap. Perhaps I should have brought more snacks with me.

Here on this hillside, a milestone. I'm about to dig in and see what I have to work with, listen to what this book might become. I earnestly cross out words in a trance, circling sentences and looping arrows toward other sentences, reworking this paragraph and that one. The first chapter is good enough. The next chapter, I doubt whether or not I should write this book at all. How can there be so much enthusiasm and struggle in a single morning? I've only been here for two hours. I slide the pages back into my folder and walk toward the lawn, diverting my thoughts to the blossoming bougainvillea and tranquil streams of the Getty's intricate gardens. Alone on a bench, I peel a tangerine, break into each juicy segment with my back teeth and watch as girls take selfies by the tulips and families push strollers away from the sun.

I can't manage more editing, so I walk inside the gallery to my favorite corner of Impressionist paintings and stop in front of Cézanne's *Still Life with Apples*. Gazing at the glossy fruit ready to tumble at any moment, my whole body feels like the apple and the blue vase atop the rumpled tablecloth, teetering on the edge of the table, suspended in air by nothing but a brushstroke.

A few days later, I'm distraught. So much of what I've already written is useless. I shuffle around for two days, thinking how to make it better. Over dinner, I announce I'm being too hard on myself. "About your book?" Andrew asks. "Yeah, it just occurred to me today. First drafts are supposed to be messy. I probably need to stick with it and keep reading."

The first draft is sacred. Beware of forgetting its true purpose: to serve as a guide. It dips our toes into cool water, gets our heart pounding and our mind racing. Although we radiate with hope as those early words breathe life into our ideas and set the foundation for things to come, the path is not always smooth. The Season of Beginnings leaves us particularly vulnerable as words are strewn among pages like autumn leaves fallen to piles. We brace for more truth-telling, the enormity of it all. We write without any promise of having something worthwhile to share in the end. But continue walking, as slowly as you need, into all that is messy and beautiful. Once you've taken the first steps and written the first words, the only way out of the forest is through it.

The Season of
Self-Doubt

If self-doubt has a strong grip, there's emotional digging to be done. One way to remedy this season is by rewriting the myths we tell ourselves and pushing aside limiting beliefs that keep us from the page.

The more important a call or action
is to our soul's evolution,
the more resistance we will feel
toward pursuing it.

—STEVEN PRESSFIELD

The Fifth Chakra

I tell my acupuncturist, Sun, I need my voice to speak at an event in two days. I tell her about a dry cough that's lingered for three weeks, and all the usual remedies I've attempted: eating raw honey, sipping tea, gargling warm salt water. Phlegm has been making its way out now, I hope, to leave my body permanently. I ask if I have too much heat or too much dampness, if it's my spleen, home to anxiety and stress. I show her my tongue.

Sun inserts thin needles with a fast, confident motion into the pillowy space between my thumb and index finger, the insides of my ankles and ears, the top of my head, more pricks in my wrists, then she sets the round warming light over my abdomen and leaves me for forty minutes. The lights are off, and a mystical, melodic flute plays from the speaker on top of a cabinet. A small indoor fountain trickles, drowning out the noise of an occasional plane flying overhead.

I close my eyes, place both hands over my stomach, try to breathe. Forty minutes used to feel like an unbearable amount of time to be still, but this was before I became a mother. Now I hope to drift off to sleep, sneak a nap, use the time to meditate, count my inhales, and feel the weight of my body sink into the cushioned table.

A few days ago, Andrew told me as gently as he could that I've been moody lately. And negative. And that our conversations seem to be mostly about what we don't have. I do this sometimes, spin my mind into a frenzy, which makes moving through even an ordinary day feel all the more difficult. That night I sank into the couch and scrolled tiredly through my Facebook feed, and a plea from a member in one of the groups I belong to caught me: "Does anyone have any thoughts about your fifth chakra being blocked? I've had a cough that I can't explain." *Of course*, I thought. This space in the throat, owner of communication, timing, and will, has been compromised. I'm pushing too hard and not listening enough. My body knows this to be true, and my mind, slowly, is beginning to trust this too.

I walked into the kitchen and stood in front of our wall calendar, tracking my days backward, recalling when the cough first started. Once I realized I should be writing a book about creativity, the thrill lasted about a week before self-doubt arrived. As soon as I opened my first blank document to start describing what this book might become, I heard the voices, nearly audible, from somewhere deep in my bones. *You have no business writing this book*, they said. Ever since the phone call with my agent, and ever since drafting my proposal, fear has led every action, every thought.

My first instinct used to be killing fear swiftly, like how I've stepped on a silverfish in the bathroom or followed it darting along the tile with a piece of toilet paper. A silverfish is attracted to dampness and darkness. Self-doubt is attracted to writers.

Lately I find little use in attempting to scare self-doubt away with a dose of rage. And ignoring it doesn't solve the dilemma either, because self-doubt will return again and again the longer you write (and you will be writing a very long time, I imagine).

It's best to address the fear with as much love as you can muster. Once you do, letting go might be immediate or it might take you days, weeks maybe. There's no rushing this.

I'd scheduled the emergency acupuncture appointment to help get my body's energy moving in the right direction again—it was an act of kindness toward my fear. Before leaving, Sun writes down an herb, loquat, to help with my cough. She's run out but says Whole Foods might carry it. My flight leaves early tomorrow morning, so it's too late to order online, although something tells me I won't need it, that I've started setting my voice free.

Making Friends with Your Amygdala

The life coach Kate Swoboda says fear is a wound. If that's true, we harbor scars from all the times a parent told us writing wasn't practical, or a teacher marked up our essays, or a fellowship application was denied. But these wounds often come from the outside—someone else's opinion, an editor's taste, and our own assumptions overcome us. Fear slides in when we're most vulnerable, making us wonder whether or not we're even a writer. (We are.)

And what's happening on the inside? There's the amygdala to contend with, an almond-shaped mass in each hemisphere of the brain that I've heard referred to as the seat of fear. The amygdala's job is to activate our flight-or-fight response in stressful situations and help us discern how to react, which is useful in emergencies but less useful when we're sending pitch letters into the void or working through a first draft. The journalist Kate

Murphy suggests reframing the amygdala as the seat of anticipation instead. "If you can sense and appreciate your fear—be it of flying, illness, or social rejection—as merely your amygdala's request for more information rather than a signal of impending doom," she wrote, "then you are on your way to calming down and engaging more conscious, logic-dominated parts of your brain." So the next time you're uncomfortably reclining in the amygdala's cushions, feet propped up, say hello to the little almond asking for help and see if you can lend a hand.

Whenever my amygdala gets the best of me and I continue to doubt my creative instincts, I go to the beach. Crashing waves lure my mind open, and I look out into the vastness of the sea, releasing a silent prayer or plea. Once, the sea made an offering: *listen and let go.*

-Rituals & Routines-

NAME YOUR FEARS

There's power in naming our fears and reclaiming gusts of confidence. It's one of the best chances we have at overcoming self-doubt and allowing our fears to turn from wounds to scars, which, given time, will fade. And if all else fails, wait for the seasons to change. When the air shifts from thick and humid to crisp and clear, renewal is never far behind. Leaves turning and trees blossoming always remind us of the potential for inner transformation—what's possible, what's within reach, what idea is worth following, and that we're able to grow wherever we're planted.

I'll go first. When I dreamed about writing this book and heard voices telling me I should be doing nothing of the sort, I let them say their piece. Then I wrote down what I was most afraid of.

I'm afraid I won't have time to write.
I'm afraid my voice isn't worthy.
I'm afraid people will pick it apart.
I'm afraid I won't have anything insightful to say.
I'm afraid to share stories I've never told anyone.
I'm afraid it won't be good enough.

If the inner critic becomes too loud to ignore, take a few minutes to list your fears, removing them from your body in the process, at least temporarily.

Hi, I'm a Writer

The first time I introduced myself as a writer, out loud, in public, in a room full of nonwriters, was more than twenty years after I started writing. You would think someone who's been a writer for as long as she can remember would be more courageous.

My husband and I were attending a benefit dinner for a local nonprofit. I was six months pregnant, wearing a flowy blue dress and sipping sparkling water from a tumbler as we circled the restaurant, bidding on auction items. Eventually someone turned our direction, and when she asked me what I did, I said I was a writer.

Since I'd recently written an article about the organization, it was a logical time to announce it. But I consciously chose not to mention how I also worked at a family foundation coordinating the world's largest humanitarian award. I was simply a writer, and it felt good.

On the way home, I wondered why I've always been reluctant to claim the title of "writer" and came up with a couple of reasons. First, writing was never front and center, which I attribute to receiving very clear messages about writing as a teenager: Be practical. It's a great hobby. Find something else to pay the bills. Save for my English teachers, I didn't know many writers to serve as role models, so my options felt limited to getting my teaching credential or moving to New York City to live in a studio apartment and eat canned tuna for dinner.

Second, I wasn't widely published and my food blog wasn't well known, so keeping my identity quiet also protected me from answering dreaded questions like, "What have you written?" or "What's the name of your book?" As true as these reasons are and while it's easy to blame them for holding me back, I also believe it takes time to grow into yourself. These are my obstacles to overcome and stories to rewrite, and I'm working on it, embodying daily who I'd like to become.

-Rituals & Routines-

CALL YOURSELF A WRITER

Calling yourself a writer sounds straightforward enough but can prove complicated out in the open. We all default to job titles, and in such settings as conferences or other professional events, of course, this is more than appropriate. Your challenge is to seek out an opportunity to tell someone you're a writer. It doesn't matter if you don't have a single publishing credit to your name or you can pull several books of yours from the shelf, we've all silenced ourselves before ever uttering a word. Tell the manicurist, the hair stylist, the stranger sitting next to you at the airport, the couple you meet on vacation and will never see again. You might find this exercise to be a helpful antidote to self-doubt, because once you start telling other people you're a writer, there's a good chance you'll start believing it too.

Send Your Breath There

Writers are storytellers by trade, yet when it comes to our *own* stories, we become mythmakers, or myth believers, or both. We convince ourselves the narratives are true and often swim in their depths long before we ever realize they're holding us back. I've done this for many years, and while it hasn't been comfortable to revisit the experiences I'm about to share with you, it has been enlightening, and freeing. How might we help release self-doubt's tight grip? By knowing what's real and what's not. I'll show you what I mean.

I hadn't been working at the museum long when I found out the annual gala was approaching and my department was in charge of the event. One of my responsibilities was to comb our database and pull member reports to create invitation lists, but somewhere between highlighting the names of VIPs and printing address labels, I saw an opportunity to help write the new invitation copy. The previous year's theme was circus-related, so I latched on to the whimsical language and tried to emulate it.

A few days later the board chair arrived for a meeting and sat down with the grants manager to chat about the invitations. The two of them read through my draft, which I'd left on a communal table in our workspace, and took turns saying how terrible it was and that they'd have to rewrite it. There was also occasional laughter. Although I was fairly certain neither of them knew I wrote it, I couldn't help but sink into my chair and attempt to distract myself with all those address labels I needed to stick onto envelopes. I wished more than anything I'd written a better draft, and I also wished for the moment to disappear from memory.

But when I set out to support other writers wading through the sea of self-doubt, I had to go back and do the same work I was asking of them. I had to identify my own myths and memories, and see them for what they really were. Something transpired in the room that I was utterly blind to in the moment: A grant writer (whose job is to solicit money from patrons) was likely hoping to impress a board chair and make it clear that she did not, in fact, write this awful invitation copy. That part doesn't have anything to do with me. Where it gets personal is what happened next. For years I succumbed to a pattern of hesitating to jump in and use my writing skills in the workplace. I downplayed my abilities and bought in to the myth that I could never be a good copywriter, but the truth was much simpler: I didn't have enough information to do my job.

I didn't have a brand guide, relationships with the board members, or any insight into how they wanted to position the event that year. For a long time I believed I was incapable of writing professionally. I have more of these stories to share, but we'll return to them later.

I've learned something through yoga that's helped me work through memories like this. While holding a pose in class, there's usually a nudge. *Deep breaths*, the voice reminds. I'm supposed to be hearing the steady roar of the ocean in my throat, but I often forget the most basic need for slow, continuous breath. "See where there might be some discomfort," the instructor says. "Just notice it, observe it. Now, send your breath there."

I'll scan my body, then find a tight spot in my neck and open my lungs again. I take it as a reminder for both the mat and the page. We don't like discomfort, so when we breathe into these memories, the ones we'd prefer stay buried or simply vanish, instead of letting our stomachs clench, we should try inviting in some oxygen. Send your breath there. Send your pen there. Write it out, think through it, and get to the core truths of these stories so you can stand a little taller. Our stories are not here to make us feel small and insignificant but to help us carve a sturdy path in stone, not sinking sand.

-Rituals & Routines-

MYTHS AND REALITIES

I can't promise that once you see myths for what they truly are, your writing life will magically transform and you'll never doubt your calling to put pen to paper. However, if you tend to your writing wounds, something will shift. That's because any time we own our stories and dedicate some real effort to uncovering emotional blockages, insights arrive. So when you doubt yourself (and you most likely will) or have a rough week where you feel like you can't put one coherent sentence together or another rejection slip arrives in your inbox, you can open up a new page in your journal and sort it out.

STEP 1: The Memory. Write down what happened and identify emotions you felt in the moment (such as insignificant or unconfident, perhaps). Once it's down on paper, you can start to see the memory from a more expansive view.

STEP 2: The Myth. What's the story you're telling yourself? Try to be specific, like *I'm not a good poet* or *My family doesn't support me as an artist*. (I once felt this way after overhearing my dad say he didn't understand why I was going to graduate school. But when my first book came out, he bought so many copies that Amazon wouldn't let him post the five-star review he drafted.)

STEP 3: The Outcome. Now it's time to clarify what happened after this experience occurred. Did it change how you moved through the world? Did it keep your voice small?

STEP 4: The Reality. Finally, let's discover what's actually true. Was it a lack of information, a misunderstanding, a case of not being in the right place at the right time, or assumptions you're projecting on to another person?

This might not be an enjoyable exercise, but it's an important one. Before you go ahead, here's another example.

THE MEMORY

I slid into a desk against the back wall and tried to look studious, pen and book in hand, which I hoped would prevent me from needing to contribute anything to the conversation. That afternoon was my first undergraduate literature seminar on a topic that didn't interest me (I've long forgotten it). It was simply the only class in my major still available on the day I registered. But I haven't forgotten red ink marked all over my first term paper. *D. Plagiarism. See me.* Immediate emotions included fear, confusion, and embarrassment. My heart sank into my stomach like a stone.

THE MYTH

The new narrative quickly became *I'm a terrible writer, I won't pass my first college class, and I'll have to move back in with my parents.*

THE OUTCOME

Hands shaking, holding my poorly written paper, I approached my professor after class and walked with her to the parking lot. As the sea breeze whipped through my hair, she pointed out my mistakes. I objected, tentatively, showing her my citations, pointing to the parentheses and page numbers. This didn't satisfy her. Apparently, I hadn't done it right, and she recommended a free course taught by the university's writing program.

My writing wasn't the problem; I simply needed to learn a new skill. I attended the training class, and it taught me everything I needed to know about writing college essays.

To begin working through your own myths, the best thing to do is set an intention to uncover some of these difficult memories. Maybe a few sprang to mind while reading my own accounts. It's also likely your memories will surface in the coming days and weeks as you devote some energy to pondering your journey so far. Whatever comes, write it down as soon as you can. The quicker these memories are identified, the sooner you can free yourself from their grasp. And a final note: it might help to remember the word *humiliation* comes from the Latin word *humus*, meaning soil or ground. "When we are humiliated," the poet David Whyte reminds us, "we are in effect returning to the ground of our being."

The Lost Voice

I did something I shouldn't have. It began innocently enough, while researching comp titles for my proposal, which is customary to explain what sets your book apart. Naturally, I started reading and revisiting several books about writing and creativity, and believed there was room for us all. But once the proposal was finished, I didn't shelve the books right away. I just kept reading and ordering new ones. Research, I reasoned! If I was to write a book about writing, it would be good to know what everyone else had done. It would be good to read all the books.

And that's when I began doubting myself for the second time before barely making any headway on the first draft. As I questioned whether or not my story could (and should) sit alongside those who have come before me, I realized what was really going on. I couldn't hear my voice. I was so far away from it, my confidence had recoiled completely. When we're struggling with our work, we're often caught in what everyone else is doing, what's been done. That makes it hard to create, to listen in. Isn't that how it goes? Enthusiasm consumes us. We're resolute. We're writing, we've started, the mess that it is will not be judged. And then we're suddenly convinced writing is a very bad idea. Once I closed the books, stopped checking Instagram so much, and reminded myself I'm the only one who can tell my story, it's become easier. Not easy, but easier.

Thank You for Your Submission

I took a publishing workshop my sophomore year of college, joining a group of eager undergraduates to learn what it would take to see our names in print. On the first day my professor set a thick manila folder on the table. "I brought you my rejection slips," she said with a smile. Some were hand cut, where an editor had designed four forms to a page to save paper. Others were printed on extra-thick yellow cardstock. A few were handwritten and even thoughtful, with a note of encouragement. Others simply read, *Thank you for your submission. Your work is not a good fit at this time.*

I came away with a few tips about literary magazines and agents, but I learned more about exercising patience, and to keep a little distance between your work and other people's opinions of it. Our words will not always find a home. Our message will not resonate with everyone, so there's no use in taking things personally when a story isn't chosen for an anthology or a poem doesn't win a contest or an anonymous reader leaves a negative blog comment.

When rejections arrive, there are a few ways to keep from internalizing it. The first thing to do—and this starts when the envelope is sealed or the email is sent—is to think of the work as being no longer yours. You were the messenger, and now the message is ready to be spread to others. If the piece isn't right for a publication, it doesn't mean *you* are not right as a person. Go back and make a few more edits, or submit the story elsewhere. Rejection is simply another chance to revise, see the words with fresh eyes, and improve. Elizabeth Gilbert has a refreshing take in her book *Big Magic*. "It's the writer's job to complete the work; it's the agent's and editor's job to decide whether the work is good enough to be published. Your job is only to write your heart out and let destiny take care of the rest."

Also, if you're concerned no one will ever publish your book, here's a story I often laugh about now. Before I had a contract for *Eat This Poem*, I wondered when my turn would come. One day I came across a collection of essays written by cats. And this book was published! Sold in a bookstore! I might not have known when

I'd see my own book on the shelf, but that moment helped me believe in the value of my idea. If the cats can be published, so can you. (Besides, your story is probably far better.)

FIND THE GOOD MEMORIES

My grandfather once told me when he couldn't sleep at night, he thought about the good memories our family shared growing up, like remembering a trip to Egypt or dancing at my wedding. I've started doing this at night too, but it's also a useful practice for the writer's life. We've done a lot of work uncovering difficult memories, so let's do the opposite now. And a note of reassurance, in case you need it: if coming up with a few examples that don't involve criticism or disappointment feels unattainable, you can thank something called the negativity bias. Our brains have evolved to be especially sensitive to unpleasant news, which means you'll remember one scathing comment from a workshop critique instead of the positive feedback that inspired your rewrite. Don't rush. Instead, let your mind know you'd like to go deep into its memory stores, and see where it leads. Write out your good memory and then list the emotions it brings up for you. (I left a few of my own below.) Once you have an archive, you can turn to them when doubt starts creeping back in.

MEMORY: SECRET DOORS

My sixth-grade teacher Mrs. Moore dimmed the lights after lunch, and we pulled notebooks from our desk cubby. I was

working on a novel about a girl who could travel through time by playing chords on a piano that unlocked a secret passageway to the past. The piano was in an old, abandoned house that once belonged to her grandparents. I didn't get very far, and the novel I was writing was no more than a handful of pages, but those afternoons felt like magic, retreating to the interior of my mind, wherever it took me.
Emotions: happy, curious

MEMORY: SUNRISE WITH THE FISHMONGER

I woke up in the middle of the night to write a story about fish, driving to a warehouse in downtown Los Angeles at dawn, where the floor was glinting with freshly shaved scales and fish still stiff from Japan waited in crates. Later that morning, I met the fishmonger at a local restaurant and interviewed him with the chef, checking my phone often to be sure it was still recording our interview. My eyes widened when a bowl of ceviche arrived, set atop custard and garnished with edible flowers. I walked back to my car, tired but grateful, the taste of the sea still on my tongue.
Emotions: confident, empowered

My Voice Is Already Here

The first thing I do in Seattle is walk down to Pike Street and look at the water. I duck into a cheese shop to devour a bowl of hot tomato soup topped with fresh curds, then move a few doors down to order a big cup of creamy yogurt swirled with fresh passion fruit. It starts raining, so I head back to the hotel, licking my spoon with one hand and angling my umbrella with the other.

The next day, I indulgently sleep in until 8:15 a.m., then take myself out to breakfast and sit uninterrupted in a coffee shop for an hour, sipping green tea and finishing the book I started on the plane. I feel rested for the first time in months. Mind open, throat clear, body at ease.

When my cab driver asks what I'm doing in town, I tell him the truth: I'm on a book tour. "You wrote a book?" he asks. "I've never driven an author before." He takes me to Book Larder, a charming cookbook store in Fremont, where they're making my rosemary brown butter popcorn and setting up chairs. I read headnotes and share the floor with my friend Megan, who guides our conversation around writing and creativity. Someone raises a hand and asks about balancing writing with a day job, and I tell her the only thing that's kept my writing afloat when it could have very easily capsized: You must never stop trying new things. You must trust in your story, be kind to yourself, and find a way.

Listening to ourselves might be the real secret, but even two days ago, half asleep on my acupuncturist's table, I still didn't believe my story was worth telling. Memories rushed in out of order, I couldn't hear myself think. I was frantic and I knew it but hoped the muse would indulge me and speed up the process a bit, accommodate the hasty timeline I'd assigned myself. She's done no such thing. But deep down, I know what to do. I must believe that my voice is already here, waiting. I roll my shirts and place them into a mesh cube, then take a hot shower and recite those words to myself as I massage shampoo into my scalp, clearing my throat in a plume of steam. *I am enough. I am enough. I am enough.*

-3-

The Season of
Going Back in Time

*Whether you've been away from the page for a spell
or are simply in need of creative refreshment, consider
this season a rest stop in the writer's life. Pull over,
spend some time uncovering your origin story, and
reconnect to the writer you've been all along.*

The most powerful tool most of us
possess is our own voice.
Take that away and what do we have?

—JOYCE MAYNARD

A Lost Notebook

I'm looking for a notebook, the one I scribbled poems and songs in when my family drove on long stretches of California highway and stopped at campsites along the coast. An advertisement might read, "Missing: One-inch-thick notebook, spiral-bound, hot pink, belonged to a ten-year-old." I didn't throw it away, and I'd seen it a few years ago at my parents' house when I was sifting through boxes from my old room. At least I thought I'd seen it, but maybe I stuffed it into the bottom of a cardboard box when we last moved.

Every shelf and drawer has been checked, and it's wishful thinking for the notebook to appear so easily, just as I'm embarking on the task of tracing through my past, written in pencil, to years when wild words first sprang out of me. The last place to look is the storage crate above our cars in the basement garage, and since it's Saturday afternoon and Henry's up from his nap, we descend, helping our son hold the railing as he eagerly marches down the stairs.

"What's the code again?" Andrew asks. The lock is the same one I used to latch my old high school locker, its black enamel face still painted with a coat of clear, glitter nail polish. It was the thing to do back then. "Fourteen, twenty-three, five," I say. Then quickly, "Henry, stay close to Mommy. Don't run behind the car!" The lock comes undone with a quick tug, and Andrew reaches overhead for a box and sets it on the cement. I open the lid, optimistic, but the notebook isn't here. Henry picks up my worn copy of *The Writer's Diary* by Virginia Woolf, then drops it on the floor, and I pull out a collection of poems by John Ashbery to bring upstairs.

I text my mom, a last hope. "The next time you're at the storage unit, can you look for a box of my old journals? I need it for something I'm working on." I'm hoping it's there among relics—an old dresser, theater scripts, and extra copies of literary magazines I edited. Storms flooded the room a few years ago, and I lost my high school yearbooks, handwritten messages blurred like every memory of those years now. I want to know if the journals survived, and if they did, I'm eager to revisit some of my earliest lines once formed from sheer impulse. These days, it might be good to remember the sensation of writing unhindered, unconcerned with editing or rejection slips or fear, unburdened by time constraints or commutes. There's something electrifying about it, knowing somewhere in a box my creative history waits for me, preserved in time.

-Rituals & Routines-

FIND YOUR LAKE

Recalling early writing memories and experiences that have shaped your origin story is a useful exercise at any stage of the writer's life. This short visualization is a way in, to nudge your subconscious into helping you along the way.

When I'm trying to remember something important, I like to imagine I'm standing in front of a lake. It's late summer, and I'm holding one hand over my eyes, peering out at the horizon. Wind lifts and a section of hair whips around my neck. This lake is my mind, cool and deep. When I'm ready to begin, I walk in slowly, feeling fresh water wrap around my ankles. The lake's surface sloshes in the wind, my memories bobbing in the distance. I stand here as long as I can, digging my toes into the sand, waiting for one of the translucent waves to splash my legs. If the memories don't come, I'll return tomorrow. I'll go back the next day, until they meet me. When I don't squint or force anything, and often when I'm moving through the day—no longer standing in front of the lake but driving my son to preschool or spotting ducks on a walk or waiting in line at the grocery store and mindlessly glancing at magazine covers—that's when I find what I've been searching for. Arriving doesn't always mean clarity, at least not right away. Visiting the lake simply means you're ready.

Make yourself comfortable, close your eyes, and try to find your lake. You can also journal or freewrite about what you're hoping to uncover.

Something I Once Believed

Now let's sit down with a cup of tea (or coffee or hot chocolate if you prefer, but a warm beverage). I'm writing to you from my corner of California and realize you might not be in the same state or time zone, but if we did happen to chat about things we haven't thought about in years, we'd want to be sipping something. On second thought, maybe pour a glass of wine.

When I was seventeen and writing poetry, I harbored a visceral fear that if I stopped writing, even for one day, I would lose my ability to do it. If you'd asked me about my creative process, it went something like this: *Write, write, write. Scribble lines on napkins and envelopes, whatever I can find. Act on every feeling, capture every word.* I didn't know my creativity well enough to understand there would be periods of waiting and trusting, so I wrote furiously every day, pages of poems, notebooks filled to the brim. One afternoon I walked across the quad to my next class, anxious because it had been approximately three days since I'd written a poem. Would I ever write again? I honestly didn't know. You can imagine how overjoyed I was when I felt charged, creative energy surging again. Pen met paper, and fear, for a moment, left my body.

The Season of Going Back in Time isn't like the others. It's not circumstantial or bookended by life events. It's a season you enter consciously, with the promise of receiving a gift I consider a walking stick, something to keep you steady on the writer's path. Going through the exercise of uncovering your origin story and knowing how you became a writer can encourage you, even on difficult days, or during a stretch of time when you don't write a single word. Instead of being hard on yourself, come rest on the shore. The memories you trace will tether you to this calling, always reminding you that the impulse isn't going anywhere.

-Rituals & Routines-

BECOME AN ARCHAEOLOGIST OF MEMORY

Now we're going to dig. I like to call this process becoming an archaeologist of memory. Put your hands in the dirt, feel around, take a water break, look again. Remember, we're here together, with our wine or our mugs of tea on a cozy couch. And there's always the tranquil lake to visit whenever you need. Maybe close your eyes and go there now, with this question in tow: When did creativity begin galloping through you like a horse, so fast that you couldn't stop it?

Maybe you remember the exact moment, or nothing at all. All you're doing now is starting to gather a few glimmers, then one day when you're chopping up a bunch of parsley or walking from the car to your dentist's office, you'll remember something your fifth-grade teacher said or a book you loved or the name of a poem you read on the inside flap of the program at your great aunt's funeral. Think of the men and women outside in the desert heat, bent over, brushing bones. When they've found something but before they know what it is, the diggers crouch down with tools and quietly and methodically strip away the dust, revealing what's been buried.

To construct a writing timeline—everything you can possibly remember about your creative history—agitate your mind by answering a few of these questions. Don't worry about assigning dates yet, just record the answers.

Have you ever admitted your creative impulse? Who did you tell, and what response did you get?

When you were growing up, what messages did you receive about the role of writing in your life?

Which teachers encouraged you? Who in your family supported you?

What experiences have you had, positive or negative, that have shaped your current beliefs about creativity?

What are some books that left an impression? What do you remember most vividly about each of them?

When was the first time you shared any of your work with anyone?

What did you write early on—poems, stories, something else? Has it changed over the years?

When have you sent your work into the world—submitted a piece for publication, read at an open-mic night, started a blog?

Have you won any contests or received any awards for your work?

Have you written a poem or story in response to a challenging personal experience?

Has someone ever gifted you a book, insisting you read it? Or have you ever gifted a book to someone else, insisting they read it?

Do you remember the first rejection letter you received?

Have you ever used your writing to help others in some way? While volunteering or at a job, perhaps?

What poems or passages have you memorized?

What were some of your favorite courses in school? Do you remember any topics, teachers, or moments that inspired you?

Remembering where you started may take time, and some days standing in the lake water will be enough. Clarity will come. When a memory floats in, and I'm certain it will, pick it up with your hands, dry it off, and add it to a list you can refer back to.

RETRACE YOUR STEPS

Once memories begin to emerge, start putting things in order. In the coming weeks sort through your answers to the questions above, along with any other flashes of memory, and construct a timeline of your creative history, similar to a portion of mine below.

1990

Built a reading fort out of blankets and spent afternoons reading Mary Higgins Clark and Michael Crichton mystery novels.

1992

Submitted stories to children's magazines and collected a first round of rejection letters.

1995

Designated family historian on summer vacations. From an old travel journal: *Friday, June 23, 1995. We left our house at 4:28 p.m. and stopped at Mobil for gas. We're on the 10 freeway heading east to stay at Buffalo Bills in Stateline, Nevada, where they built the tallest and fastest rollercoaster*

in the world. . . . The buffet at Whiskey Pete's was awful—they
didn't even have ranch dressing.

1996

My best friend Marissa moved away the summer before
we started high school. I wrote a short story to process my
feelings but changed everyone's names.

1999

Edited my high school's first literary magazine and
devoured confessional poetry.

2002

Published my own chapbooks for a class assignment by
going to the campus copy shop and saddle stapling pages
of printed poems together.

2004

A college professor and mentor, Barry Spacks, read "The
Day Lady Died" by Frank O'Hara to our workshop, maybe
six of us. At the part about picking up a hamburger and a
carton of cigarettes, Barry's deep, raspy voice quivered.
By the time he reached the line where we see Billie's face
on the cover of the *New York Post*, Barry stopped and
softly asked the student next to him to finish reading the
poem. Having been alive at that moment in history, he was
transported back decades, undone. He didn't apologize

or sweep his feelings aside, he simply allowed the swell of
emotion to burst through.

2008

Rushed into the hallway when an Iowa phone number
popped up on my screen. It was the editor of the Iowa
State University Press telling me I won its annual chapbook
contest. Started my first blog.

Another Kind of Lake

There's the lake of the mind, where we can visit to remember
things. And there is Walden Pond in Concord, Massachusetts,
where I visited the summer before my senior year of high school.
It was part of my family's official American History Tour—three
weeks driving through the northeastern United States in a rented
minivan stuffed with thirteen pieces of luggage.

We started in Washington, walking for miles in the July heat
and taking respite in air-conditioned museums. In Virginia, my
mom sprained her middle finger. At a stoplight in Charlottesville,
she and my brother decided to quickly trade places so he could sit
in the front seat. They unbuckled their belts and rushed into the
street, climbing back into the car as the light turned green. My
mom reached for the sliding door and swung it closed, but her
other hand was still gripping the outside of the front door, so the
sheer force smashed her finger. Instead of driving to the University

of Virginia (this was also an unofficial college campus tour), we drove to the closest hospital.

The three of us sat in the waiting room while her hand was X-rayed and bandaged. I was bored but brought a notebook with me. When I stood up to go to the water fountain, a young girl followed, searching for a friend. I wrote about the afternoon in my journal, and maybe even a short story. That's what we writers do—keep our antennae up, scribble notes, draft pages and pages, and see what's there in the midst of our days, odd as they might become. An hour later, my mom walked out from the double doors and we finally headed north.

The next stop was Massachusetts: Plymouth, Boston, and Concord. The pond was calm, and as we walked along the edge, passing swimmers and families, I thought about what it might be like to live deliberately in the woods. I'm reading *Walden* again now and making slow progress in the few minutes before I fall asleep at night. I'm a terrible reader these days. Drifting off, I'm thankful we're not measured by how many words we write, or how swiftly, but simply whether we are making an effort, doing what we were made for.

Have you ever wondered if not being a writer would be easier? Or what it might be like to move through life without noticing every detail, asking as many questions, or recording every idea that arrives, half formed, in your mind? I have. But we can't wish writing away. We can smudge but never erase our yearnings. Since we must keep writing as best we can, as often as we can, honoring our creative history is one way to help fuel the work. Maya Angelou said there's "no greater agony than bearing an untold story inside of you." Promise me right now that instead of casting your stories aside, you'll find the courage to tell them.

WRITE YOUR ORIGIN STORY

While we're on the topic of courageously telling our stories, let's begin with how you discovered writing in the first place.

STEP 1: Look back through your writing timeline and single out one of the earliest writing memories to expand on.

STEP 2: Set a timer for five minutes. Turn to a blank page and explore this period as much as you can.

STEP 3: Repeat two or three more times, until you've expanded on a few memories.

STEP 4: When you're finished, you can keep it to yourself or polish it for posting on your blog or submission to a publication.

My Origin Story

I've been a writer for as long as I can remember. More than running, tap dancing, painting, kicking soccer balls, or singing in school musicals—all activities I participated in while growing up—writing was always an effortless pursuit that felt as natural as breathing.

I learned my cursive letters in Mrs. Day's second-grade class, when I was seven, which is about the time I also started imagining stories and creating rhyming songs, like a catchy tune for grape-flavored Juicy Juice. I even recorded the jingle, and my parents sent it to the company's headquarters to use for their next commercial. We never heard back from them.

In high school, the need to write became impossible to ignore. My second-period English class walked to the library together to check out dusty copies of the *Norton Anthology of Poetry*. The pages smelled musty, like a home that needed its windows flung open to let fresh spring air inside. With our books and bodies spread out on the classroom floor, my teacher asked us to flip through the book and stop on the first poem our eyes landed on.

Softly, in the dusk, a woman is singing to me;
Taking me back down the vista of years . . .

It was "The Piano" by D. H. Lawrence, who described sitting under the instrument as a young child, pressing his mother's poised feet as she sang softly above the "boom of tingling strings." I was lured by the rhythmic lines, the longing, and the idea that a melody could move you through memory. I wrote my own poem that night, the first real poem I can recall, and didn't stop for nine years.

In college I bought my very own paperback copy of the *Norton Anthology* for a class whose only assignment that quarter was to read the entirety of the tome, all two thousand or so pages. I haven't looked at it in ages. I place the book on the dining room table with a thud, it must weigh three pounds, and think of an old professor, not more than five feet tall with short red hair. She wore oversize skirts and dark burgundy lipstick and carted a dictionary to class so we could look up words we didn't know the meanings of. A few of my term papers are stuffed between the pages, and I unfold one, read a version of this origin story, which means I've been trying to tell it for nearly fifteen years.

What I Was Looking For

My parents have come to babysit so Andrew and I can meet friends for dinner. Bearing gifts, my dad walks through the door carrying a brown cardboard box. I sit on our tufted chair in the living room with the box on my lap, glancing at a few of the books he brought for Henry, holding up a new copy of *Little Blue Truck*. "Oh, he'll love this," I say. "We can show him when he wakes up from his nap."

"There's something else," he says. An unmarked manila envelope sits at the bottom of the pile, rumpled. I open the flap, and there it is, like a treasure, my pink notebook still marked in thick black ink with loopy handwriting: *Poems 1992*. The corners are slightly worn. I smile. Suddenly I'm decades younger, asking my pencil to keep up with my mind, writing songs on family vacations in Malibu, recording our daily activities, like how we spent the day bike riding and played a rousing game of Uno by lamplight after dinner so loudly that other campers asked us to be quiet. In the morning my mom made pancakes with Bisquick batter and bacon on the side before we grabbed our boogie boards and marched off to the beach.

One morning we stopped at the dunes outside Sycamore Canyon's campsite first. My friend Kira and I played in the sand, tucked oversize T-shirts into our soccer shorts, and scooped in piles of sand, filling our bellies, looking round and pregnant. Then we started climbing, stopping often to look back and see how far we'd come. The reward was taking in the view—something we wouldn't have seen if it weren't for a few minutes of effort, heavy breathing and all. Having done it, we tumbled back down, somersaulting with our eyes shut, laughing hard before landing at the bottom of the hill.

-4-

The Season of
Discontent

If you're railing against a set of frustrating circumstances—as we all do from time to time— transformative mind-set shifts will help release blame from your job, family, and anything else keeping you from the page.

Transformation doesn't ask that you stop
being you. It demands that you find a way
back to the authenticity and strength that's
already inside of you. You only have to bloom.

—CHERYL STRAYED

Walking in the Desert

There's a poem by W. S. Merwin called "Air," where he writes about walking in the desert at night, and his lines brushed up against my heart like a soft wind.

> This way the dust, that way the dust.
> I listen to both sides
> But I keep right on.

Don't you love when the right words show up at the right time? This poem must have known I needed to read it. It was 2013 when the family foundation I worked for relocated its offices thirty miles outside of town, ushering in a long Season of Discontent. In Los Angeles, the land of highways and SigAlerts, miles matter, and there was no pretending that driving sixty miles instead of four every day wouldn't deeply affect me, it was only a matter of how and when.

In the early days a new rhythm emerged marked by gentle bumps vibrating under my seat as I drove north every morning just after sunrise. But after a few months of misty-morning commutes, I felt the first pangs in my lower back. The throbbing usually started on my drive home, when I alternated between listening to Audie Cornish delivering the day's top stories on NPR's *All Things Considered* and KNX1070's local traffic reports.

A few months earlier, while we packed our desks and shredded old documents, something extraordinary happened: I got an email from an editor asking if I'd be interested in developing my food blog into a cookbook. So in addition to labeling boxes, I was also trying to think about *that*. I wanted to think about it constantly. I tried to keep right on, straddled between two worlds—a world where suggesting something as minor as changing a brochure font took weeks of tenacity, and a world where I was writing a book. In both worlds, change was painfully slow, which didn't sit well. On more than one occasion, the Tuesday morning editorial meeting with my potential publisher was pushed back or cancelled due to sickness or Boston snowstorms. On days I didn't receive a regretful cancellation message from my editor, I refreshed my email obsessively, hoping for news. I was making myself crazy. I was most certainly, indisputably, lost somewhere in the desert.

The First Thing to Do: Make Peace

Making peace with your circumstances is challenging work. A concerted effort must be made to uncover old storylines holding you back, and then you must endure the experimental phase where you try on different mantras and methods to help you cope. You will most likely have days that seem promising, and others that seem futile. All entirely normal, I'm afraid. And maybe the hardest part of all, peacemaking involves embracing something that feels like surrender, which you might not have a history of running toward with open arms. (I certainly don't.)

When you know what's required to shift your mind-set, the misery can be more appealing at first. Writers are experts at lamenting challenges delaying our progress. There's comfort in assigning blame elsewhere, isn't there? It doesn't matter whether you make a living with words or by using other skills, we'll always grapple with the tension of never feeling like we have enough time to write, so we begin resenting everything else.

The Season of Discontent can be a deeply unsettling place where negativity reigns and feels at odds with who you know you are inside: a writer with things to say and words to write, yet somehow shackled. Although, after floundering for a few days (or a few months, as I did) with knots in your stomach and anxiety in your heart, you'll realize the frustration you've been blindly following around has revealed nothing useful except that you'd be better served without it. This can be difficult to believe in the moment but is always a relief in retrospect.

Something that keeps me optimistic is knowing others have gone before me. On a Dear Sugars podcast episode, Cheryl Strayed and Steve Almond called up George Saunders to ask how he and his wife were able to pay the electric bill and also support his creative pursuits while raising a young family. Over the years, George had a series of tech writing jobs, and one day at the office it occurred to him that if he was to call himself a writer, he should be able to find material for his fiction there. And you know what else? Even now, with all his literary success, George still struggles to get those four or five hours a day he needs to write. None of us is immune.

This is what I needed to hear at twenty-two, fresh out of college and hoping to make a way for myself. Yet hearing the conversation only last year also confirmed what I'd come to believe: all life experiences are useful. They exist to teach us something, and if we're paying close attention, these periods offer inspiration and support in return.

OBSTACLES AND OPPORTUNITIES

One of the hardest aspects of hovering in The Season of Discontent is resisting the urge to lament the circumstances, which can become second nature, almost as comforting as curling up in a blanket. But give this a try. First, make a list of the biggest obstacles you're facing right now. It might look something like this:

> Lack of clarity on what to write about
> Lack of time to devote to writing
> A long commute
> Fatigue
> Parenting obligations
> Bringing work home with you
> A desire to change jobs

Now, look for opportunities to shift your mind-set. How can you use these obstacles for good? How can they serve you instead of the other way around? Can you play an inspiring podcast on your drive? If you take the train, can you read or draft poems? Can you arrange childcare for a couple of hours on the weekend, so you can get away to write? Do you need to change jobs immediately, or can you stay awhile? You don't need all the answers now, just a few ideas to start considering.

The Second Thing to Do: Make Priorities

Reconciling my career and my creativity has been a struggle since the day I graduated from college and went on my first interview for a teacher's assistant position at a local charter school. I had very little idea what might make me happy back then, followed by a series of jobs that never felt quite right. I'm grateful in hindsight, because my discontent led to blogging, which led me to my first book, which has led me here, helping you avoid my mistakes.

I was working as a media researcher at a public affairs firm in Santa Barbara and spent my early mornings scanning newspaper headlines and articles for mentions of our clients. The office was quiet. Some days I was the only person there at 7:30 a.m. before the coffee machine hissed or the phone started ringing. I packaged the day's stories into custom templates, saved them as PDFs, and emailed them to our distribution list.

One night our friend Adam was over for dinner, and I casually mentioned I didn't feel fulfilled. Graduate school had ended, and I wasn't writing much. But I was cooking, and Adam wisely suggested I start a blog. *Cooking After Five* was my first attempt at developing recipes, photographing everything we ate, and telling stories through the lens of food. I made elaborate dinners like salt-crusted fish and clam chowder in our dark, windowless kitchen, and soon I was more satisfied than ever. I still went to work, but I had something else to occupy my mind.

I used to tell myself repeatedly that if I could just quit my job, life would change. Maybe you've had a similar conversation with yourself. But there are several reasons a steady job can be beneficial to writers. First, there's the matter of financial stability, which means there's less pressure on your writing life. Over the years I've started to see my career as a partner in my creativity, and welcome what my day job truly is: a patron. It's an opportunity to pursue my writing with greater freedom, rather than relying on it to pay the bills. There's also the matter of transferable skills, like learning complex software (a company once paid for me to attend an InDesign training), and I've found every job has taught me something I've taken with me to the next one, or even into my writing life. Maybe you understand the nuances of vendor negotiations, which might come in handy when you hire a designer for your website or are looking for a book editor. It all matters.

-Rituals & Routines-

ARRANGE YOUR IDEAS

In *Essentialism: The Disciplined Pursuit of Less* Greg McKeown describes the way of the essentialist, who replaces phrases such as "I can do both" and "It's all important" with "Only a few things really matter" and "I choose to." It amplified what I knew deep in my soul to be true. I needed to pare down my writing projects. It would be the only way to make space for what came next, to hear myself think, and to become a mother *and*. A mother and a writer. A mother and a wife. A mother and a senior content editor. A mother and a friend. A mother and a person who wants to be informed about the world but not overwhelmed by it. A mother who practices yoga and cooks and remembers to fill up the dog's water bowl.

I read reluctantly but was undeniably curious. "If we underinvest in ourselves, and by that I mean our minds, our bodies, and our spirits, we damage the very tool we need to make our highest contribution," McKeown wrote. In one moment, it's as simple as this: Spending time with Henry, eating, moving my body, writing—these are essential activities. Playing crossword puzzles on my phone and shopping online are not. Knowing this is one thing, but it doesn't make it easy to shift our habits.

To decide what's essential in your writing life, I recommend an exercise involving a large pad of fluorescent sticky notes. On each square, write a project you'd like to pursue, such as freelance work, book ideas, a blog series, newsletter, teaching opportunities, events or workshops, or podcast interviews. Be specific. Write down every hope, every idea, every flicker, then stick the squares on an open wall and walk away. This is important—go about your day. Glance at the wall when you pass by, maybe pause for a few seconds, but don't stop. Let yourself think and ponder, then two days later, or whenever you feel ready, ask yourself, *What do I really want?*

Once you have an answer—to write books, to grow your readership, to publish poetry, to draft a play—write it down and stick it at the top of all the squares. This is your essential idea. Next, you'll need to identify the one or two activities that will help you get there. Here's an example: When I did this for the first time, my hope was to write more books, so I made two columns for the activities I felt were essential to helping me achieve this: "Sell Copies of My First Book" and "Nurture a Community."

With this clarity in place, it's time to begin arranging, seeing where pieces fit, and determining where your energy should go. If you feel stuck or unsure, walk away again. Underneath the label "Nurture a Community," I placed sticky notes for my newsletter and Facebook group, for example. But I had a handful of notes I didn't know what to do with, like some freelance work and an e-book I'd been tinkering with. I walked away. Don't be alarmed if some ideas you stuck to the wall don't fit under your essential columns (many won't). It doesn't mean the projects won't be essential another time, but with your limited resources, choices must be made.

After a few days, you should be feeling more rooted. You'll know what you need to seek in this season, and what you need to consider letting go of. You can do this anytime you're at a crossroads, when you're wishing you could do everything simultaneously but your life won't accommodate it. As difficult as it is to let go of things you want to pursue, once you've released them you'll immediately be better equipped to maximize your margins; even five minutes of writing one afternoon will contribute to your highest purpose at this moment in time, to the story that must be told now, before you move on to the next one. And you'll feel lighter.

An additional benefit to becoming more comfortable with an essentialism philosophy is applying it to domestic tasks. For instance, if I'm sitting on the couch in the evening and suddenly realize I didn't boil a batch of eggs for Henry's lunches, should I get up to do it or can it wait until the morning? If I walk into the bathroom and see yoga pants and a few delicate tops hanging from a wooden drying rack, should I put them away or can the steaming and folding wait another day or two? It's almost always possible to wait.

Trusting What We Cannot See

I didn't go for a walk, but I made a cup of tea. My electric kettle bubbled to precisely 100°F, and I filled a mug with hot water before dunking the steeper and sticking my nose over the rim to inhale sage and dried orange peel. While I moved around the kitchen, pulling out a small gold spoon to stir in a squirt of honey, I remembered how I used to get my hair cut on the other side of town. Since I hadn't found a new salon after a recent move, it seemed easier to embrace the familiar, even if it meant taking two freeways and a few side streets to get there.

I hit some traffic on the way home, the kind where a highway patrol officer started driving ahead of us, looping through lanes, slowing down cars. There didn't seem to be an accident, which made it all the more mysterious. After about half a mile at this pace, we stopped completely. The officer parked his motorcycle on the shoulder, then walked into the center of the highway where a large piece of rolled carpet had fallen off a truck and slung it over his shoulder in one swift motion.

He soon flagged us to keep driving, and although I'd lost only a few minutes of my afternoon, the whole experience felt rather peculiar and important somehow. Picking up speed again, I realized a lesson I needed to learn in that moment: when obstacles are in our way, we need to trust they'll be removed at the right time, even when we don't see them coming.

-Rituals & Routines-

NEW MANTRA BUFFET

There are weeks or months that require a boost of encouragement, something to hold on to as often as necessary. Choose one from this list, or write your own, and put it somewhere you'll be looking: the car dashboard, the bathroom mirror, the desktop computer at work.

I'm the only one who can tell my story

My career empowers my creativity

Progress over perfection

When I write, I nurture an authentic part of myself

Seasons change

One thing at a time

The Third Thing to Do: Make Progress

In her essay "The Getaway Car," Ann Patchett tells the story of how after graduate school she left her husband and her new teaching job and moved back in with her mother in Nashville. Working as a waitress at TGI Fridays, Ann decided if she wanted to be a writer, she'd need to write her way to a better life for herself. "It was a test of love: How long would I stick around once things were no longer going my way?" This is when she figured out how to work in her head during restaurant shifts. Her brain made space for appetizer and cocktail orders, as well as characters for the novel she wanted to write.

I learned another writing lesson at a restaurant, The French Laundry in Yountville. At the end of our meal, we asked our server to see the kitchen, and she led us down a corridor, motioning for us to stand inside the door. It was immaculate and intimate, with gleaming stainless-steel counters and copper pots hanging above the stoves. The entire space was enveloped by a composed quietness I didn't expect. Sizzling and chopping was merely a murmur, yet every plate that made its journey to the dining room was consistent, well-seasoned, and the best version of itself. On our flight home, I wondered about working in that kitchen, in awe of what was cooked within the confines of a space that forces you to confront efficiency. In our writing life, it's not about having unlimited amounts of time at our disposal but magnifying the time we *do* have.

Once I decided my dream of writing a book was more important than waiting for permission, I started doing this too. On my commute, I read a poem before I got on the road so I could think up recipes and stories on the way. I became more consistent about writing on my lunch breaks, sometimes driving down the road to the closest coffee shop, and other times closing the door to my office and pulling out my laptop. On the weekends, I said no to social activities more frequently, and watched less television so I could test recipes in the kitchen instead. It was my first brush at writing in the margins. I looked at my schedule, found the pockets, and seized them as best I could. After all, our choices, not our circumstances, impact our ability to create.

During this year and a half, three things happened: I made peace with my schedule, I established a clear priority to begin writing my cookbook, and I started seeing progress both in my writing and in my spirit. It was a profound, transformative change that still reverberates through the decisions I make today. There are only three words to remember: *Peace. Priorities. Progress.* I affectionately call this framework The Writing Cycle of Hope, which provides a way forward and, as I've come to learn, is replicable. Seasons change, they do, so repeat it as many times as you need.

I Should Be Honest

I'd rather be out to brunch or getting a massage. That's my truth today, Sunday, a day I prefer to do as little as possible. Except there is this book to write and work is keeping me too busy to make much headway during the week. My deadline is still five months away, which seems like a reasonable amount of time for being on the second draft already, yet it's also uncomfortably close.

But since we're being honest, there's something else going on: I'm in The Season of Discontent. Again. After coming out the other side five years ago, I thought I'd learned the lessons well enough to keep me from teetering on the brink of despair. *Make peace, make priorities, make progress.* I know the formula, but on a lazy weekend, my resolve is being tested.

You'd think there would be nothing to dissatisfy me this time around. I work as a writer and editor for a food start-up and spend my days editing recipes, writing blog posts, and developing web copy. I have a nonexistent commute, a flexible vacation policy, and leave promptly at 5 p.m. every evening to pick up Henry from school. Even as I type this list of benefits, I realize how it sounds. My situation is good, really good. Yet there are days and weeks anchored by dissatisfaction because I'm operating within the constraints of a schedule I don't entirely control. Writing falls somewhere between work, family time, meal planning, laundry, exercise, and sleep.

I don't write every day. My energy doesn't allow for it. Or, I should rephrase: I write every day, but it's not always the writing I most want to be doing. Years ago, I would have been tougher on myself, asked my spirit to work a bit harder. Not now. So although I'm here again—new job, new life, still struggling to write consistently—at least I've weathered the season before. This time around, I'm considering my life as a poem. Not free verse lines falling where they may, but a poem with form, like a sonnet or villanelle. These feel restrictive to write at first, counting syllables and forming rhymes, my voice contained within parameters. But if I keep at it, won't I find the poem inside the shape, waiting to be born? Yes. Although some days, like today, I'd rather wallow than work. I told you this would happen: some days feel promising, like when I sit at the park during lunch and type a few paragraphs on my phone, and other days feel futile, like when I go a week without writing at all.

Yet we must persist because the reward for showing up and writing—in any amount—is exactly the antidote to our writerly grievances: progress. I saw it when one Saturday afternoon I opened the Google Doc of my cookbook manuscript and realized I had the makings of an entire chapter. I saw it when I ignored my book proposal for a week, then returned to find perfectly usable paragraphs. And I've seen for the past six months, writing fragment after fragment—often during less than ideal times—that when I started revising the messy first draft I was happy with enough of it to see me through the second draft. (Revisit the Find Your Margins exercise in The Season of Beginnings if you need.) I'm telling myself all this because it's one of those days when I probably need to simply take a walk around the block and get some perspective.

-Rituals & Routines-

WRITE YOUR WAY THROUGH IT

Writing might come naturally, but it's sometimes overlooked as a tool to help us sort through feelings. It can be as easy as journaling or creating a document for venting, if you like, but I enjoy making an "I Wish" list as a first line of defense to sort through bubbling emotions.

However you approach it, the idea is to move the emotions from inside your body to the page. Nothing has to come from it creatively. It's highly unlikely this will be the piece you pitch as a guest essay or publish on your blog. I'll give you an example of a list I would have written several years ago (although some of these items are still relevant).

> > I wish I didn't have a long commute
> > I wish I had a private office
> > I wish dinner would make itself
> > I wish I had more time to read
> > I wish my schedule was more flexible
> > I wish I could read an entire magazine in one sitting
> > I wish I could sleep in

Don't worry about censoring yourself. Write down everything that arrives and add to the list over the course of a week. Next, see which concern is the most pressing, and set out to remedy it as best you can. If you want more time to read, are there places you can make space for it? If you commute, can you listen to a book on tape, or write on the subway? If dinner is an obstacle, can you use a meal delivery service once or twice a week? It won't all change at once, but remember: progress. Even a few small shifts will help make a difference.

What I Wanted to Be Doing

After dinner one night, Andrew described the sensation of leaving an old job like visiting your college campus after graduation. It's a place filled with good memories and gratitude, but you know you're not supposed to be there anymore. On the drive home from my last day at the office, I kept telling myself I'd done it. After almost a year and a half of searching, I made this opening. Not alone, not without wisdom and grace, but I found a way out, and through the tears of leaving one chapter of my career behind I knew—even while sitting in traffic on the 101 freeway—that I was entering a new season. I shaped it. It was mine. This Season of Discontent was over.

The tough stuff refines us, makes us go to deep places, and the only way forward is to lean in to the discomfort and see what it can teach you. My commute was a teacher. My publishing journey was a teacher. It might take a long time, but one day you'll be finished walking through the desert and be able to look back on those difficult, sun-drenched days and think, *I made it across.*

At the end of his poem, Merwin realized what he wanted to be doing all along:

Walking at night between the two deserts,
singing.

Writers don't want to choose. We don't want to write someone else's words and never our own. We don't want to miss time with friends and family. But we must start across these two deserts, singing our songs, writing our words, listening to both sides, letting them mold us, making space for everything that matters. The oasis isn't trembling on the horizon, it's inside us, ready to quench our thirst. And if you're searching your writing life for something to control, there is only this: whether or not you show up to the page. This season might be fraught with challenges, but you can choose to make writing a priority. And one day, those words will lead you out of the desert.

-5-

The Season of
Listening to Your Body

Repeat after me: the body comes first. You can't produce your best work if you don't take care of yourself, and since writing is a lifelong pursuit, you must always nurture yourself along the way.

Nothing is more exciting than knowing that
our bodies and our feelings are
a clear, open pathway toward our destinies.
—DR. CHRISTIANE NORTHRUP

Whatever Doesn't Serve

I've noticed a pattern, reliable as autumn leaves falling from their branches. Whenever my writing feels stuck, or when it's been weeks since I've moved my fingers across the keyboard, my body responds. It also does this if I focus too much on things outside my control, like the time we were settling on a title for this book and I was so anxious my monthly cycle was days longer than usual.

I know when my body is cared for (and there are many ways to accomplish this), my creativity flows more freely and more frequently. I've known this for longer than I've admitted, and that's how I found myself curled up on the couch last night, trying to explain to my husband what it's like having a body that's constantly sending me messages—every day, every week, every month. I told him I sometimes wished I didn't have to think about it.

Maybe I should start at the beginning. I've avoided writing this chapter because I haven't wanted to believe that taking care of myself directly affects my creative life. I haven't wanted to consciously accept doing less or that certain writing projects may take twice as long as they used to. Although I'd prefer to draft several chapters per month, I've settled on two as the most I can accommodate without sacrificing sleep or sanity. I'm sensitive. My cells are listening.

Since Henry was born, I've been tired. Fatigue in the early weeks was real and consuming. I often dozed off while he nursed in the middle of the night. Now the new normal has stabilized, and while I'm slightly less worn out than I used to be, I also haven't been to a yoga class in two months. My body is talking, and the signs are undeniable. Muscles ache, my shoulders are hunched over. To recalibrate myself I must do the smallest acts of self-care imaginable. After dropping Henry off at preschool, I stop at my favorite juice bar for a vibrant blend of carrot, orange, apple, turmeric, and pineapple. I tote the glass back to my desk and drink it before a meeting, then schedule an acupuncture appointment. I brew tea and sip it while reading food magazines, stretch before bed, diffuse lavender essential oil, put fresh flowers in a vase, go to bed early, remove the constraint of self-imposed deadlines.

Traveling through the deepest tunnels of tiredness has cast a dim glow on something else I'm still struggling to name. Whatever it is, this force has made it clear I can't do as much as before. What began as a sadness, a strangeness, has morphed into a reckoning. I'm fairly certain that moving my body regularly will help. I tried last summer, but because of travel schedules and work commitments, the routine didn't last. When I was able to roll out my yoga mat, I often felt like I was moving through class with my eyes half shut. I held poses, but I didn't feel the energy they contained and hardly had any strength to keep my arms up. I didn't remember to use my breath or to deepen it. Emotions stayed above the surface.

These classes were at a fluorescent-lit gym in my neighborhood where the thump of runners on the treadmill could be heard from the other side of large glass doors, and occasionally weight lifters walked in with their oversize headphones and oversize muscles to grab a dumbbell stacked at the back of the room. I wanted to look these athletes in the eye and convey my silent displeasure, but instead I tried to steady my gaze on the floor while holding tree pose.

During one session, while we rested in savasana, the instructor recited a favorite poem. My ears perked up, and I opened my eyes to glance in her direction. She asked if there were burdens we could lift and urged us to let go of old stories with every breath, the ones we've told ourselves repeatedly and believed wholeheartedly. Simply let them go. One breath in, one breath out is always a place to begin.

-Rituals & Routines-

RETURN TO YOURSELF

In order to support ourselves, we need to know what restores us. Make a list of things that help you feel more connected to your body and keep it handy on your phone or in a journal, so you can reach for it whenever you need. A few things always make me feel better:

> Looking at the ocean
> Feeling wind on my face
> Petting my dog
> Eating a bowl of homemade granola with ice cold almond milk
> Reading a book to my son while he sits in my lap
> Soaking in a hot bath with Epsom salt and essential oils
> Lighting candles at the dinner table
> Going to a yoga class
> Saying no to something that drains my energy

> Meditating

> Remembering my work is not for everyone

> Recognizing my limitations

> Naming fears out loud, either alone in the car or with someone
  I trust

> Pulling a frozen brownie from the freezer

> Watching a musical

Lighting candles at the dinner table may not seem revolutionary, but you'd be surprised by how many meals are eaten without the glow basking our plates. It's one thing to know something might help, and quite another to bring our awareness there repeatedly, to follow through with the task, however small. It's never one thing that does it but a series of intentional actions over time that help bring us home.

This or That

On Friday afternoon my coworker Jillian and I walk to a sushi restaurant for lunch. She's just returned from a trip to England with her family, so I ask about the logistics of taking an eight-month-old baby on an international flight, and then we start talking about what we always talk about: how to do it all—or anything, really.

We both work full-time, we're both moms, we both have writing projects we pursue on the side, and we both dream of carving out more time to exercise. We even stop in a barre studio on the way back to the office so she can pick up a class schedule. Crossing the street, I blurt out the truth I've been wrestling with all year: I wish I didn't have to choose between writing and exercise. Once I say it out loud, I realize I've pitted these two fundamental activities against each other, forcing myself to deem one more important. I've created a knot, the kind you accidentally tangle in delicate necklaces and no amount of nimble finger trickery seems to release it.

I'm holding steady, not quite exhausted but not energized enough to span an entire day. My best hours are in the morning when my mind is sharpest, and I often wish I could take naps in the afternoon or go to the beach and snuggle my toes into the cold sand. If I give my body what it needs, I reason, it will mean less time to write. It means choosing my health over my words, but maybe that's exactly what I need to do.

On Kindness

"What ghosts or demons are you carrying, and can you reckon with them?" Above the music, my yoga instructor raises her voice and asks this question. I've never thought of my writing fears as ghosts, but maybe they are in a way, hovering between this life and the next but never quite leaving me for good.

It's Monday night, and I'm in the same studio where I did prenatal yoga, when an unnamed baby still kicked in my belly. I decide the best way to reacquaint myself with my body is to leave my gym, where the floors aren't swept between classes and where I blow stray hairs away from me during a low cobra pose.

I need essential oils and dimmer switches and classes with as few as three people.

By Tuesday, I'm soaking in a hot bath because my hamstrings are tight, and I suddenly feel abdominal muscles I haven't noticed in years. I look up the class description from last night: *An all-levels vinyasa flow class. Designed to strengthen and stretch all major muscle groups by combining breath with movement.* That explains why I was sweating—it was supposed to push me to my edge.

On Wednesday I almost don't go back because I'm afraid of not keeping up. I'll be the one in the back of the room, falling into child's pose while everyone else moves through chaturanga. But I show up. A woman rolls out her mat next to mine, and for the entire class I watch her enter poses and quickly pull herself out of them. When she stands against the back wall, I don't judge her for it. In fact, I think it's wonderful. She's listening to her limits and doing what she can. That's always enough. I sink into my own child's pose, elongating my fingers to feel a deep stretch along my shoulders, and it occurs to me I need to extend the same empathy to myself—in yoga, in writing, in life. If I can't stretch my legs as high or need to drop my knees, it doesn't matter.

Empathy for others has never been a challenge. Since I was young, I've looked at people and seen two sides to every story, wanted to understand their experiences. At one of my first jobs out of college, I took a professional development survey called StrengthsFinder, where you answer hundreds of questions to identify your innate abilities. Empathy was in my top five, and years later when I took the test again, it held. *You can sense the emotions of those around you. Intuitively, you are able to see the world through their eyes and share their perspective. You hear the unvoiced questions. You anticipate the need.* But empathy for myself? Empathy for the writer in me? That's more difficult to give, and something that must be practiced.

There's a space in my office called the recovery room. You're not allowed to hold meetings or speak but are welcome to meditate, work quietly, drink tea, or stretch. It's a haven, and every Wednesday we're led through a guided meditation by Julia, who often says to let all the parts of ourselves show up without judgment and simply observe our feelings as best we can.

She starts today's session with a story about a class she recently taught in a formal corporate building where she couldn't even use the term *meditation* to describe what she was there to do. It was a "mindfulness session" in a conference room—no pillows, no music, only productivity tips. She started talking about how stress from morning traffic can affect communication, but then a hand shot up. "How can we deal with anxiety from all the terrible things happening in the world?" The room went silent. "OK," she said. "Let's talk about that."

Of course, she didn't offer concrete answers. Meditation won't stop violence and hatred, but it *will* change something in our power to control: ourselves. She said it's OK to not know what to do, and to wait to make a grand gesture or a statement. In the meantime we can be really kind and really present with people. Some days, that might be enough to cause a ripple effect. It reminds me of the quote attributed to K. A. Laity about how a pebble starts the avalanche.

In our world, in our writing, we don't need all the answers right now. Sometimes we're better served by waiting or listening. Sometimes we need to write one word, then another, then a few sentences. We can build a mountain that way, out of words and dust and water. It may take years, but we can build one. We can always stretch and try.

-Rituals & Routines-

FOCUS ON FEELINGS

One Friday Andrew and I met for lunch at a bar in the beachy neighborhood where we used to live. We ordered drinks, shared a basket of French fries, and with the fresh breeze flowing through the front door and the promise of a weekend ahead, we felt liberated. Our conversation turned toward the future, but with a slant. He proposed that instead of listing all the concrete things we want, we focus on how we want to feel. Because our lunch felt relaxing, we decided we wanted more of that. When I'm working against myself and my body instead of with them, I try to remember to focus on my feelings, then ask two questions that can help reorient myself: *What do I need? What can I change?*

WHAT DO YOU NEED?

It's a deceptively simple question, because we rarely pause to articulate the answer. Take a few minutes to think about your body and your creativity.

What do you need to do this work, or do it better? Think internally, such as a shift in your perspective, or externally, such as a dedicated workspace in your home or a new notebook.

What do you need to support your body? A massage, a new cardio class, more sleep?

Do you need to better understand your characters?

Do you need a weekend away to finish your first draft?

Do you need to find your appetite again, for writing and for life?

Do you need a new morning or evening routine?

WHAT CAN YOU CHANGE?

With a better idea of what's been gnawing at you, let's see about shifting some things. What can you change? Think of the smallest action, because as much as you might like to leave your job so you can be a novelist, or you'd like to put your house up for sale so you can move to another with room for an office, these types of big life changes only happen because of the micro-movements that have come before them. Remember how the pebble starts the avalanche?

Write down a few ideas. Maybe try a Zumba class or plan weekly walks with a friend. Learn to throw pottery. Delete some of the television shows you're recording and read more in the evening instead. Maybe shift your mind-set around something that's bothering you at the moment. Light more candles. Buy a new tea kettle. I once shared a panel with a journalist who wrote a captivating book about her grandfather's escape from the Armenian genocide. After our talk, someone asked how she decompresses from dealing with the harrowing subject matter. Without hesitation, she said reading *People* and watching reality television. She knew what she needed to support herself. You get the idea.

A Slow-Writing Manifesto

Todd Sieling wrote a slow-blog manifesto in 2006 describing the movement as "an affirmation that not all things worth reading are written quickly," which aligns with what my body has been saying all along: slow, slow, slow. But if a less frantic pace feels like a counterintuitive rhythm, consider it an invitation to incorporate wellness into your writing practice.

Wellness—the state of being healthy in body and mind—is everywhere from magazines and blogs, to turmeric tonics and meditation apps. So how might this expansive idea have resonance for writers? Whether your version of healthy is meditating regularly, cooking vegan meals, or moving your body for at least thirty minutes a day, the result you're after will require deliberate, intentional effort. So it goes with the writer's life, where we may work unhurried, embrace seasons as they arise, and draft in margins as brief as five minutes. This is writing well. This is slow writing. And it's not the result of one short story submission or graduating with an MFA, or even a visit to the metaphorical lake to mine for memories.

Beware of coming within earshot of intoxicating internet voices shouting at you to publish three blog posts every week, write viral content, quit your job to follow your passion, or create gorgeous Pinterest boards. Instead, tune in to sharing what's in your heart when it feels good, not because you've done a deep dive into Google Analytics and discovered the most popular time on your blog is Thursday at 5:36 p.m. No, because you've been thinking about something for a while now, rolling thoughts over in your mind the way you suck on a sunflower seed before spitting out the shell. Because you've taken deep breaths and sipped hot drinks. Because you've considered, drafted, polished, and it finally feels right to watch your words extend beyond your precious care. Daily discipline—attending to both body and mind—compounded over weeks and months, reinforces habits that help us do the necessary work of storytelling, however long it takes.

Writing slowly doesn't keep pace with our social media–fueled culture, but it does steady us within ourselves. There are times when a brisker pace may be required (I'm likely to type a bit faster the closer I get to my deadline), but I don't remain here. There are energetic seasons and reflective seasons, and no matter where you're hovering, your words matter, and when the time is right, they'll be given wings.

-Rituals & Routines-

PRACTICE THE ART OF SLOW WRITING

Slow writing is grounded in the belief that less is more, our writing careers are long, and there's no rush, no race, and no reason to push ourselves to the brink of exhaustion. Or, a more succinct definition:

not doing all the things. And since your time and your health are precious assets—not renewable resources—slow writing is also about protection. To this end, here are a few guidelines for incorporating this mind-set into your writing life.

> Lead with intuition
> Take care of your body (even if it means less time to write)
> Pursue fewer projects at a time
> Do what's best for you and the community you're creating (not what an expert recommends)
> Notice trends and best practices, but allow in only what feels instinctually helpful
> Ignore anything or any person who uses the word *hustle*
> Write at your own pace
> Don't compare your journey with someone else's
> Honor milestones of all sizes, always

Change One Thing, Change Your Life

Our sponge rests on a ceramic tray on the counter, to the left of the sink. About a year ago, I was deep cleaning the house before a party, and I unplugged my stand mixer, pulling it forward a few inches so I could reach the crumbs. Everything was moved, including the sponge. When I'd finished wiping the sink, I placed the sponge on the opposite side, on the silver lip where the dish soap used to be, a somewhat insignificant change in the moment. I stepped back and admired how pristine everything was.

Later that night I picked up the sponge to wash the remnants of our meal from ceramic plates, and I placed the dish soap bottle directly onto the dish. Within seconds I realized my mistake, but it got me thinking about muscle memory and change. There I was at the sink, forgetting the new order of things because for months I'd done something one way. And if it takes a week to retrain my brain about where my sponge and dish soap belong, why am I giving myself such a hard time about everything else?

Meaningful change, the kind that we'll be able to look back on and really *see* a year or two from now, takes time. Longer than you might think. Longer than we ever want it to. When I moved my sponge, I wasn't just moving my sponge. I was in the midst of an upheaval left over from earlier in the year when we moved and the company I worked for closed its Los Angeles office and I was dealing with the reality of my baby turning one and preparing to launch my cookbook and discover what might come next. We had family in town. Our garbage disposal stopped working and took two days to get fixed. The city trimmed the palm trees in front of our building and left a mess of debris on our patio. Life was speaking, my body was recoiling. I was only days away from weaning Henry, joyful to be reconnecting with my own body again, mournful at the milestone.

I know this seems like nothing, moving the sponge, but it's a whole lot. It's bigger than cleaning, bigger than me. Life is always changing. Sometimes it's by design, sometimes it's not. The thing about email or online communities, or anything about how we interact nowadays, is that nothing is as it seems. We're not necessarily trying to be secretive, but the nature of our real lives isn't always front and center. There's more going on with you than I know. There's more going on with me than you know. The best we can do is be patient with ourselves and try to do one thing, every day, that makes us feel good. It might be writing. It might be dancing. It might be caressing your cat or walking your child to school. Change one thing, change your life.

-6-

The Season of Raising Young Children

This season is long, stretching over years, underlying all you do.
Writing can be disjointed and difficult, especially since several
seasons converge—the need for self-care, the liminal space of
transitioning from one life to the next, and, for some, feelings
of discontent as new rhythms and routines are embraced.
But as you grow as a parent, you can also grow as a writer,
discovering new ways to work, finding harmony in writing less
than you're used to, and embracing the present moment.

There is a time during one's life when, if you
are responsible for the care of your kids,
it is very hard to do other creative work. You
have to do it around the edges.

—URSULA K. LE GUIN

Negotiations

"Mommy, I play with Winnie the Pooh!"

"Mommy, I build a tower!"

"Mommy, come in!"

It's Sunday afternoon, and I'm typing in the nook off our kitchen while Henry plays in his room down the hall. Midsentence, midthought, I answer. "What do you need, bud?" I get up, telling myself he will not always be this small. Other moments, I'm not so generous and silently hope he'll occupy himself a few minutes longer.

Time is not my own. Time is not my own. Time is not my own. I've sung this anthem since the day we drove home from the hospital with a seven-pound baby snug in his car seat. I still sing it, storing these words in my heart as I fold laundry or place yogurt and chard on the conveyor belt at the grocery store, pushing the cart with Henry inside.

I understood this new life would need every part of me for a time, and the page would become like a friend who announces she's moving across the country. We'll Skype and occasionally visit each other, but our friendship is forever changed. Now there's a clearly marked before and after, like the crisp fold of a letter. I anticipated it all, though after wearing sweatpants for two weeks, eating muffins pulled from the freezer, and forgetting what day it was, I was ready to write again. But there were restless nights, and an overwhelming two-hour struggle to introduce a bottle when I wasn't producing enough milk. There were uncontrollable sobs on my last day of maternity leave, facing down the thought of having to turn and walk in the opposite direction of my child for eight hours. Each of those challenges have passed now, and it's taken me years to find a new rhythm.

After the contract for this book was signed, I declared with confidence that I wouldn't be able to finish it without uninterrupted time. Where might I find some? I did the thing I rarely do: ask for help. Andrew and I talked about digging into our weekends, my leaving the house, and removing the need to make dinner some evenings, or dust.

So here we are. Words arrive one sentence after another, two paragraphs at a time, in thirty minutes on my lunch break, and in notes typed on my phone after crawling into bed or before turning off the car and walking through the gate at preschool. These are my margins, where books are born and writing is raised. This life-altering season has forced me to confront everything I thought I knew about what serves my writing life, and make radical adjustments to keep pursuing my art.

Even if you're a formerly self-sufficient and fiercely independent person, to write and to parent, you'll have to adapt. Collaborate with your partner and try new things. When your infant starts daycare or your toddler drops the second nap, make shifts and discover what works now. I won't pretend it wasn't odd to ask for something—the gift of time—that was once mine in abundance, but for the next several years your writing progress might very well depend on whether or not you ask for what you need and then set out to get it.

A Womb, a Bridge

In one moment you stand impatiently in the bathroom where two blue lines form a bridge to carry you from this version of your life to the next. You know everything will change, yet nothing has. A baby is growing but has yet to be born. Many women have waved the stick around, inspected it, made sure what they were seeing was true, then rushed to the other room to start making plans and start panicking. Months go by, and then you favor a nap over something else, or try to write and the baby—who you tenderly swaddled and sung to sleep—wails. You have walked across the bridge now.

Until the baby arrives, you only experience this in theory. You're caught between your past life and the new one to come, the arc of your growing belly reminding you day after day how far away you are from your former self, both physically and creatively. Know that writing may flow with the trimesters—words feel burdensome in the first, you're energetic and bursting with ideas in the second, and, finally, in the third you simply curl under blankets and say no to everything. At the end don't be surprised if there's a rush to conclude anything that's remained unfinished. Blame hormones or the urge to nest, but if anything, use pregnancy as practice for taking cues from your body, consuming instead of creating, and restoring yourself. It won't be the only liminal space you encounter (there's an entire chapter coming up about that), but it can help you get comfortable with the necessary skill of adapting and feeling content with the idea of changing the course of creativity in the coming months.

Perhaps the best advice I can offer anyone preparing to enter this season is: wait and see. If you prefer systems and strategies, parenthood is unlikely to be contained in a spreadsheet or a single book on newborn sleeping advice. Conversations around bodily functions will dominate your days, that much is certain. The rest needs to pause. There's no way to know if you'll have a baby that sleeps through the night at six weeks or six months, or one who cluster feeds in the middle of the day or cries the moment you set him down and walk away. You can't foresee how long it will take your body to heal from labor, or how many days it will be before you cook a meal for yourself, or what you'll feel like writing (or not). This likely isn't news to you, but sometimes it's helpful to hear it again from someone who's a bit further along.

Don't bother with word counts or weekly blog posts or any of that. It's one more thing to reach for or be hard on yourself for, when really you should be doing something radically simple: see how you feel moment to moment, day by day. Write because you feel like it, because it makes you happy, or because a good line flashed in your mind out of nowhere and needs to be remembered.

The first writerly activity I did as a new mother was type up my birth story while Henry napped in a swing. But after that, I had no capacity to write blog posts or tweets or newsletters. I did schedule some of these things in advance, which I recommend, but you can also forego them entirely. My maternity leave coincided with the final stages of preparing to deliver my first book to the publisher. The manuscript was written, thankfully. That's when I stood in my living room and read the Mary Oliver poem

I told you about and looked around at my life, realizing things could not be as they were before.

I should also tell you this: no one mentioned the first year after having a baby would be a grieving period. It's easy to ignore the shedding of your former self, especially when there are diapers to be changed and baths to give, and also when there is so much good and so much joy. But if you feel any twinge of sorrow as you attempt to reconcile your previous life with a new version you're not entirely settled on yet, sit with it, write about it, and know this is part of the delicate process of becoming a parent.

A podcast host once asked me if I hadn't become a mother, if I'd still be creating as much as I did before. Without hesitating, I told her yes. I'm still capable of following through, doing the work, and being strategic, but in reflection, I'm able to see how much energy I wasted on things that didn't matter. I was often spread thin, passionate but not focused. For all its challenges, that's the gift you'll receive in The Season of Raising Young Children, if you haven't already—to get abundantly clear on the stories worth telling, the activities worth pursuing, and the courage to set aside everything else.

-Rituals & Routines-

FIND YOUR MARGINS: PARENTHOOD EDITION

Silence, a room with a door, or a coffee shop might sound like a dream. But when we can't achieve our ideal writing day, there are still many ways to make progress, even when the writing feels fragmented. Remember the power of writing in the margins, and that it all adds up.

> **BRING A NOTEBOOK INTO YOUR CHILD'S ROOM.** Henry has a wall of pillows and stuffed animals, so sometimes I recline and write for a few minutes while he plays with his xylophone or jumps on his trampoline.

> **SCHEDULE A WRITING DATE NIGHT.** I've experimented with dedicating an evening or two a week to writing, ideally on a night when Andrew has some extra work to bring home, so we can sit next to each other and be productive, nibbling pieces of dark chocolate.

> **CAPTURE IDEAS CONSTANTLY.** When I have an inspired thought—a line for a poem, a topic for a newsletter, or a theme for a blog post—I write it down. The notes keep getting longer, but some days it's all I can manage. The most important thing is to not let the thoughts disappear, because there's no guarantee they'll return.

> **EMBRACE TECHNOLOGY.** I'm happy to write on my phone when necessary, which is where first drafts often originate. This proved useful in the early days of motherhood when I sat on the couch with a large pillow wedge around my abdomen, feeding my son. If I had an idea, I held the phone with one hand and pecked at the keyboard with the other or attempted a one-handed approach that took twice as long but also worked. When your child is in the infant stage, a phone is a tool that's usually within reach, so you can start there.

In speaking to many writers over the years, I've gleaned a few additional ways to support a writing practice in this season.

> Go to the library
> Sit at the same Starbucks table during every lunch break
> Write after your kids fall asleep
> Write before your kids wake up
> Book a hotel room for one or two days to finish something
> Write in the car while waiting for band practice to end
> Keep a dream journal by the bed
> Jot down poetry lines while dinner bakes in the oven

Writing or Bread

A food ritual: On Friday I open my small gray notebook and make a list of meals for the following week. On the opposite page, a shopping list—one column for the farmers' market and another for the grocery store. There's usually a bit of room left at the top of the page, so I also write a to-do list of sorts, ambitions for the weekend or things to make in advance, so I can save time in the coming days. Soak and cook beans, make salad dressing, bake honey oat bread, blend cashew milk.

Eating breakfast this morning, I'm on the verge of tears. Between bites of pancakes I'm contemplating cooking tasks and settling our weekend plans of going to the park and meeting a friend for brunch and cleaning the house and doing four loads of laundry. And writing. "When will I make the bread?" I ask. "You don't have to make it this week," Andrew offers. "Just buy a loaf at the market."

But I want to make bread. In fact, I'm longing to make bread, not because of the nutty smell but because it signifies a life I'm not currently living, one where I have hours to wait for dough to ferment overnight, rise on the counter, then rise again, to shape the loaf with my hands in the afternoon, bake it for an hour, then wait for the bread to cool before slicing into the crusty top and spreading it with salted butter. Some weekends I don't have to decide between baking bread or writing words. Others, I do. Andrew's right this time—someone can bake the bread for us this week. No one else can write for me.

Stay the Road

Last spring I drove down to Laguna Beach to speak at a local bookstore. Andrew and I planned to go together, just the two of us, but things changed when a last-minute business trip was put on his calendar. Early that morning we strapped our son into his car seat and drove to the airport to drop Andrew off. Merging back into the traffic circle, I tried not to cry. "Daddy go to the airport?" Henry asked. "Yep, Daddy will be home in a few days," I said, a tear rolling down my cheek. A few hours later he was thirty-thousand feet in the air, flying to Stockholm, and I was driving down the 405 freeway while my parents stayed with Henry. I was alone.

It was a kind of freedom, welcome after a restlessness I'd been feeling for weeks. One day I was overcome with an urge to drive to the desert, somewhere hot, and stare at the plants who survive all year in the heat. This tightening comes occasionally, and I convince myself the only way to loosen it involves driving far away. It seems I received my wish, however brief. After parking on a side street, I walked straight toward the water.

The event was better attended than I'd hoped—twenty-five people, most of them strangers. My face felt hot when I started reading from the introduction, but several paragraphs in and steadying myself against the table, I relaxed. I thought of nothing else in that moment except poetry, stories from the kitchen, and making eye contact. My in-laws came down from Bakersfield, so after I signed books we walked next door for a scoop of gelato before I went home. As I drove into the sunset, the hills lining the highway were covered in yellow wildflowers, and Glen Hansard was singing "Stay the Road" through the speakers, with lyrics all about taking time to look back and see how far you've come.

I played the song twice, then a third time, singing along, fighting tears as I had earlier that morning. At the end of each chorus was a reminder that the work is just beginning, and I realized when we're open and free and sharing our words, it's not the end of anything at all. As the light lowered and I veered toward LAX, the city looked drenched in gold.

We're led to believe physical freedom is the most desirable— the ability to whisk ourselves away whenever we please, drive anywhere, fly anywhere. But as a plane landed overhead and I heard its thunderous engine echo in the Sepulveda tunnel, I felt content, home. Being inside that bookstore was restorative. I was immersed in being a writer first, a mother second. I don't need to drive to the desert, or never check my office email again, or remove all deadlines or responsibilities in life. What I need is more telling the story only I can tell, more hearing the collective sigh of an audience who feels a poem's power in unison as I speak the last line, more standing on cliffs and looking into the sea. I need this as often as I can get it. And I was free today because of the page, because I've kept writing all this time, and will fight to continue doing it. *The Yellow House* blog put it this way: "People are wrong when they say you need to be brave to get out of your comfort zone, travel, and see things. The travel and perspective—the escapism, really—are a privilege. The real courage is needed at home, when the ordinary things don't change unless you work to make them so."

Turning the key in its lock, I entered my home, moved among the stack of dishes in the sink and the meetings on my calendar for the next day. These are not chains. Henry nibbling at homemade macaroni and cheese is a moment I want to soak up, like every night we eat together around the table. No, not chains, but links to what matters most.

-Rituals & Routines-

KEEP A ONE-LINE-A-DAY JOURNAL

It's a little after 8 p.m. I'm rereading *Bird by Bird* by Anne Lamott and doze off right at the part where she tells her students to write toward the emotional center of things, to risk being vulnerable. I know it's a season, and some days I happily give up my time to read books with Henry or watch him push a small red convertible through a wooden car wash. I don't hesitate in those moments, but it means the writing is slower. It means thoughts take longer to form, and I always feel a little bit tired and in a position of having to favor one important thing over the other. In these years, the way to survive is through grace, and the radical need to be gentle with ourselves.

It's a directive whispered by my soul while I meditated one evening. I recently started practicing yoga nidra, and on the second day an intention rose sharp and clear: *I am gentle with myself and others.* All this time the truth was so buried it was barely audible. Lying down, I heard myself for the first time in months, maybe even a year. Everything depends on kindness.

When writing feels impossible, even maintaining a consistent journaling practice, there's another way: one line a day. I adopted this routine several years ago and am thankful because it helps me remember my life. Try it, and I'm certain you'll appreciate keeping a record of your days, even the harried ones.

The easiest method I've found is keeping the journal bedside to write in before falling asleep. If you notice several days (or weeks) going by, rely on your phone. Anytime you think of something to add, type it up, then copy the daily notes in batches when you have some spare time, or every Sunday evening to keep things consistent.

Please don't feel as though every sentence should be eloquent, insightful, or even grammatically correct. If it's easier, write in lowercase, forget about periods. No one will see this but you. I tend to vary my entries between quotes, food I ate, something my son said or did, or how I'm feeling. Again, overthinking is the enemy to the one-line-a-day method. Here's what I mean about keeping things simple.

Read in a magazine: "Life's too short to bother with creative work that doesn't make a fire in your mind, body, and soul."

Today's mantra: cook, write, repeat.

Plucked two gray hairs from the top of my head. They looked like violin strings.

Hot. Traffic. Yoga. Reading old poems. Worn. Hopeful. Need to recharge. Lesson: Listen to your body.

Today's wish: a good night's sleep.

From yoga class: "Love your limitations, because they will change."

Tough commute day.

Grateful for sunshine.

From *Yoga Journal*: "A ritual is an action that is performed regularly with conscious intention."

You always have permission to write more than one sentence if you're inclined. One sentence is simply the minimum to record a detail from your day, but there will certainly be times that warrant greater exploration.

One of my favorite rituals at the end of the year is looking back through the notebook, recalling the experiences, challenges, and wisdom that marked my days, challenged me, or lifted my spirits over the past twelve months. If anything, it'll remind you how far you've come.

Everything Is Birthed in Time

A Pocket for Corduroy by Don Freeman was a favorite book of mine growing up, perhaps because I also had a teddy bear that I slept with and carried around. One Christmas I almost lost him in a crowd while my parents pulled me and my brother in a wagon to look at twinkling lights in a nearby neighborhood. Somehow the bear tumbled out of my arms, and once I realized he was gone, I started crying uncontrollably. My mom ran back to find him, which she eventually did, so I could easily relate to the story of temporarily misplacing a favorite stuffed animal.

But there's a lesson about creativity inside the book's pages, too, which I overlooked until recently when I started reading the book to Henry while he sat in his high chair nibbling on banana slices. The laundromat is almost closing, and Lisa and her mother have left to go home. Corduroy, on a quest to find material to sew a pocket on his overalls, wanders off, and Lisa's mother promises they'll come back in the morning to look for him.

The bear burrows himself in a bag of wet laundry, and a man discovers Corduroy just before tossing his pile into the dryer. We learn the man is an artist, and as he waits for the clothes to dry, he pulls out a drawing pad, fascinated by the mosaic of colors tumbling behind the dryer door. The artist is doing something ordinary, a chore, yet still returns to his studio with a fresh sketch and a new idea.

I know this works because today I've accomplished nothing on my to-do list, but I did write three sentences. Three. I tell Andrew this over dinner and he laughs, reaching for a high five across the table, sweetly celebrating the achievement with me. In the rush of plating bowls of rice draped with red lentil curry, I forgot to open the wine. It's leftover from last night, enough Syrah for each of us to have a glass. Neither of us bothers getting up, but after I wash the dishes and Andrew starts giving Henry a bath, I pull down a small tumbler and pour my share.

In the living room I shove our ottoman against my chair and place my feet on top. The wine goes on a coaster beside me. Sometimes all you need is a different view. Henry's splashing water, Andrew's singing *Row, row, row your boat*, and our dog's quietly licking her paw in front of the fireplace. I smile. I write until I hear the call: "Mommy! Mommy, come tuck in!"

So many days are both beautiful and challenging, but you *will* emerge from the fourth trimester, from the first year and every year after, and you'll still be able to write. It will be different, though in many ways, it might even be better. And remember: A woman is born with microscopic eggs stored in her ovaries. Moments old, she already has everything she needs to create. Her body, by design, was made to gestate ideas, stories, life. We are creators. Every month, our body reminds us of this fact.

If you're rocking a newborn and afraid you might not write again, or if you're awake at two in the morning warming a bottle, unable to devote yourself to anything but feeding your child, know that it will continue to be new and difficult, maybe for a few years. This season will ask you to change, do less, pull down fewer books from the shelf, and store ideas in notebooks. But think of the forty weeks you waited patiently, growing a person in your womb. You managed, and then you brought life into the world. Your ideas might stay buried in your creative womb space, but everything is birthed in time.

The Season of
Liminal Space

Welcome to The Season of Transition. You're neither here nor there but in between, which can feel like scissor kicking underwater, keeping your legs moving so your body can stay above the surface, eyes darting until you see where you need to go. It's never easy, but there are unexpected benefits— growth, change, and restoring your creative soul.

May your trails be crooked, winding,
lonesome, dangerous,
leading to the most amazing view.
—EDWARD ABBEY

Writing without a Compass

Can I still call myself a writer?

This isn't the question I thought I'd ask myself only a few months after finishing graduate school, but I quickly went from a writer who wrote to a writer who didn't, so I wasn't sure how to refer to myself. At all of sixteen, I decided the only way to become an official Writer with a capital *W* was to get an MFA in poetry and, by twenty-four, I'd done it. A degree doesn't make the writer, though; it just supports her to write better and stronger. A useful two years, yes. Necessary? Maybe not. But when you're young and fixated on something, there's no changing your mind.

On a crisp January day, after walking across a stage in Vermont and accepting my diploma, Andrew and I went out to lunch at a restaurant run by the local culinary school. We ate grilled fish and drank white wine before flying to New York for a few days. Back home in California, the concern about whether or not I was indeed a writer had not only settled somewhere in my body but vibrated throughout the summer. Wildflowers bloomed on the hills, but my creativity gradually went dormant.

Has poetry abandoned me, or have I abandoned poetry?

The season offered signs that emerged only in hindsight. The first and most obvious marker was my graduation date circled on the calendar, signaling an abrupt end to academic life. The first few months of transition were the hardest, shifting my days from sitting in coffee-shop chairs to desk chairs, trading four hours a day in the office for eight, coming home tired and hungry. Soon renewals for *Ploughshares* and *Poetry* lapsed. Emails between old professors became infrequent. I no longer spent afternoons sitting on the floor, poems sprawled in a half-moon shape around me, drafting cover letters and affixing postage on self-addressed stamped envelopes. To save space in our apartment, books were placed in boxes and sent to live in the carport. For as much as I gave up, parting with *Poets & Writers* magazine felt impossible, with its classifieds I once circled in orange highlighting, eager to send poems into slush piles. I thought if I kept letting issues stack up by my bedside table, I might still be a writer.

Other signs were subtler, like feeling an ache to write more but not being able to muster the words. Poem fragments were left unattended in notebooks, and if I polished any, it wasn't anywhere near the eight or ten per month I wrote during graduate school. And although I won a contest and published a chapbook, I was unequipped to support myself during this season, so I mostly stopped writing. It is my deep hope to help you avoid the same fate.

There's a name for the place I was, and the place you may be: liminal space. It's the time between what was and what comes next. I learned about liminal space on a podcast by the author and former pastor Rob Bell, where he shared how he and his wife coped after dropping their son off at college. "Central to being healthy and alive is understanding—and then embracing—the dynamic temporal nature of life," he said across the airwaves. Finally having a name for this murky experience softened me completely. Even saying the name out loud, *liminal space*, the *m* forcing my lips open slightly to push out a breath, felt comforting, knowing there was some order in the chaos. Or if not order, at least a dim light up ahead.

To help you find your footing, some practical matters: This season can be brief or long, planned or unplanned. There's often overlap between your personal life and creative life. In some liminal space, writing thrives, and in others, it withers and waits. Above all, it's a period marked by some kind of transition.

Liminal space in your personal life might be planning a wedding, pregnancy, maternity leave, packing up your house to move, or searching for a new job. These are periods with known endings, where you can plan ahead a bit. Then there are always situations that catch us by surprise, like family emergencies, ending a relationship, or a sudden career opportunity that takes you across the country. Sometimes writing beckons, providing a respite from other demands or simply an emotional outlet while you cope. One friend wrote her cookbook while waiting for an adoption to come through, each recipe spread like a balm of protection over her heart.

On the creative side any academic graduation can usher in a season of liminal space, as can the first few months after publishing a book. These are predictable seasons, but what about when we slip into a fog, are moored in self-doubt, or experience a setback, like a book rejection from a publisher you hoped to work with, leaving your story without a home? (Naturally, this news may arrive while you're stuffing books into boxes for that cross-country move.) You see, there's really no telling all the ways liminal space can thread itself through our lives.

My parents gave me a check for two hundred dollars as a graduation gift when I finished my MFA. I deposited the money into my bank account, then promptly went to Williams-Sonoma to buy a seven-quart Dutch oven in a soft white shade called Dune. I cooked soup in that pot, baked bread in it, stirred sauces, seared meat. It became an emblem of the season when I traded poetry for cooking, following my hungers into the kitchen day after day. When I started my first blog, I'd never written about food. I learned as I went, followed my intuition, told stories peppered with mentions of cilantro and a series of baking disasters. I was an apprentice again, as I was in high school a decade earlier, when teachers gave me poetry books to read and I went to coffee-shop readings downtown with the college kids, ordering hot chocolate at the counter instead of black coffee, clutching my paper cup in the dark.

It hadn't occurred to me that the transition from student to budding professional would require a rearranging of my creative life, so I often scolded myself for everything I wasn't accomplishing, for not being the writer I thought I was. Except, no one taught me anything about being a writer in the world. No one handed me a compass and said to point it north. Yet this liminal space altered my writing for the better and led to my first food blog, which led to my second, which led to a book. When I stopped reading and writing poetry for three years, I didn't know its absence would be the fuel I'd need to start EatThisPoem.com. I was just hungry after a long day's work. The benefit of this season is tapping into curiosity. If I hadn't recognized I missed poetry but didn't know what to do about it, I would never have found myself alone in the hallway, reading an old poem, thinking I could turn it into a recipe. Openness fueled all of it.

Think back to some of the periods of liminal space you've encountered. Perhaps you never named them in this way. If you look at where you began, you might realize, despite the surprising turns, you eventually ended up where you both needed and wanted to go. The new job, the book contract, the positive pregnancy test, the article pitch finally accepted. You will get there, like I will get there. Liminal space is not about the outcome but about the journey, which means emerging from this season will require transformation. It's natural to resist it, but we can also rest in it.

A secret of this season, I've found, is to welcome the uncertainty, because our souls can change here. In fact, it's where creativity can begin too, like how we trust that roots are growing in rich soil long before sprouts push through. Sometimes I think liminal space exists simply to remind us how little we can control, and how important it is to turn inward. I want to tell that young girl to be kinder to herself and to trust the long stretches of silence. Are you still a writer? Why yes, of course you are. You're just in the eye of the storm that hasn't calmed yet. Hold on.

Mantras you might like to borrow:

Accept what is
I am content with uncertainty
Wait in peace
Listen, breathe, repeat

I am hopeful for the future

I am curious to see how life unfolds

-Rituals & Routines-

PERMISSION TO PAUSE

This season might shine a harsh light on where you are, but liminal space is a gift. It can help you discern what to let go of or set aside, and provides time to think, an undervalued necessity in the writer's life. This exercise is something you can do alone in the pages of your journal, or in conversation with your spouse or a close friend. Try it if you find yourself in the middle of liminal space or right before it begins. The purpose isn't to bring the season to an end but to help you face it as confidently as possible, like when Julia Child looked into the camera, knife in hand, bird on the counter, and said, we must confront the duck.

Ask yourself, what type of liminal space are you in—personal or creative? (They may overlap.) Is this period something you can prepare for, or have you been blindsided by unexpected circumstances?

Sort out the details by explaining what's happening. Your daughter is about to leave for college, or your father-in-law was hospitalized as you're starting to edit your book of short stories, or you've submitted applications to six MFA programs and are eagerly anticipating the next chapter.

Next, identify any creative potential. Are you still able to work, perhaps with an altered schedule, or is it best to set writing aside until you're through this period?

No matter what you're up against, liminal space gives you permission to pause. If this season is defined by straddling what was and what's to come, then there's simply no way around making some kind of shift, even a temporary one, when it comes to your writing routines. Table your words, as needed, until old routines normalize or new routines surface. And please don't forget that liminal space can be both happy and sad. Change is always a form of loss, and since this season will cause some upheaval, either internally or externally, or both, notice your emotions. They're simply telling the truth about how you're feeling and need a soft place to land.

Consume vs. Create

Liminal space is a kind of winter. The author and entrepreneur Kate Northrup calls it the fertile void, a season marked by rest, gliding into the unknown, pausing, and reevaluating. "Deep, true creativity doesn't emerge despite the deep pause; it emerges because of it," she wrote. Float outside of your body and your life. Hover over it. Feel everything.

You need space to breathe and sometimes to lovingly set aside whatever you're working on. Yes, of course you may pick at pages here and there, like a small bird. You may journal if it helps. Don't ignore the call if a line arrives in your head or an idea drifts by. Take comfort in this place of refuge. If you're spending your days packing up a house to move, get lost in a novel. Catch up on all the blogs you used to read before you became so engrossed in writing your own. Simply savor other people's work without feeling the pressure to create. Until you're ready, that is.

Become a tourist in your town, sit in a dark bar and listen to live music pulsing in your body, indulge in five-course meals, read a pile of magazines in one sitting, take your child to the beach and watch them laugh at the waves. Wait, tend to your life, and then you'll write. Another way to cope with liminal space is to seek out opportunities that you'll look forward to. Feed your soul in all the ways you know how, trusting that seasons always end.

The first year we moved to Los Angeles, a coworker told us about a series of film symposiums that take place in the week leading up to the Academy Awards. Because my husband makes video games for a living, we started a tradition of attending the animation symposium, which we did for four years until our son was born. I don't have a particular interest in animation as an art form, and I've never been good at drawing. (I was jealous of a girl named Maureen in my third-grade class who was alarmingly gifted at rendering anything she saw into detailed colored pencil sketches.) But although animation isn't my creative medium, I'm always eager to surround myself with passionate people, no matter the topic, and in the dimness of that theater, there was palpable energy, a contagious fervor. Directors introduced favorite clips and shared the personal memories they lent to their characters, utterly committed to the craft and telling the most compelling story. I always walked away feeling lit up from something that had nothing to do with my writing life.

When we couldn't go this past year, we watched *Ratatouille* one night with Henry. After he went to bed, I turned on the special features and something stood out. The writer and director, Brad Bird, said people make mistakes thinking they can force ideas to come. All we can do, he said, is simply observe what kind of environment puts you in a creative state of mind and work to re-create it. So take stock and make plans. Seek it out. You'll find inspiration in surprising places. And even if you're still not writing, at the very least it will reinforce the belief that creativity is alive and well in the world.

Because liminal space can be quiet creatively, writing can feel eclipsed when you're between projects, facing a dry spell, or adjusting to new life circumstances. But there are opportunities in the darkness. Think of rinsing beans or peeling potatoes. The routine of doing monotonous, predictable kitchen tasks can free your mind to wander while you work with your hands. Erin Boyle writes about this in her book, *Simple Matters*, where preparing food becomes a kind of loosening. "Half of my writing gets done while chopping vegetables, which is to say: I churn the sentences over in my brain as I cut into a head of cauliflower." All the more reason for writers to nourish themselves well so words might follow.

-Rituals & Routines-

FEED YOUR CREATIVITY

During my junior year of college I took a class on Impressionist art led by a visiting Monet scholar. Over the course of the semester, he illuminated every brushstroke, painting these artists as deep observers who could look into a puddle after it rained and find beauty in the mud and the worm that crawled to reach dry land. I often think of this after a storm.

That same year, my literature seminar went on a field trip to the Santa Barbara Museum of Art with an assignment: find something that moves you and write about it. We fanned out in all directions, eventually settling onto the benches and opening our notebooks. This exercise is a wonderful companion to liminal space, because it helps find new sources of inspiration.

STEP 1: Wander through the galleries of any art museum and see what colors or portraits compel you to reflect a bit longer than the others.

STEP 2: Choose a piece of art to start with, one that draws you in, and stand in front of it for a few minutes. Don't reach for your notebook yet, just let your mind wander, make connections, and ask questions.

STEP 3: Find a comfortable seat and ready your pen. Start a poem using the title of the painting, or see if the subject might inspire a short story. Draft a journal entry or a memory that occurred a few weeks or a few years ago that suddenly feels important to work through. Maybe you simply need to remember what it's like to allow someone else's art to penetrate your heart for a moment.

Sometimes it seems creativity is more about our openness to the process than our desire to create. I believe this because inspiration is everywhere. In puddles, paintings, out the window of an airplane, the sunrise on a morning commute, or chopped onions glistening in a hot pan, surrendering to heat. The beauty will go on. It will always be available. What matters is whether we acknowledge it, capture it, and use it in a way that invites even more beauty into our lives and that of anyone we might share it with.

It Never Goes According to Plan

After exactly sixteen weeks at home with my newborn, maternity leave came to a close. The night before Henry's first morning at daycare, I sobbed after putting him to bed. And as I began navigating the realities of functioning as a working parent, The Season of Liminal Space—which so far had included all of pregnancy and the fourth trimester—was abruptly lengthened.

I remember the spring afternoon so clearly, with its bright sky, salt in the breeze, and a vibration in my pocket as I walked the half mile from our condo to my acupuncturist's office. It was a little past noon, and when Andrew's face popped up on my phone screen, I figured he was calling on his lunch break to talk, but he didn't even wait for a greeting. "We have to move," he blurted out. He told me why before I even had a chance to ask. Our landlords wanted their son, a recent college graduate, to move into the condo we were renting. Our two-year lease was coming up for renewal, and we naively assumed we'd transition to a month-to-month contract until the time came to put in our notice. Except, we were being evicted and needed to find a new home in the next sixty days.

Henry was five months old, starting to pull his head up and roll his body over. While sipping glasses of zinfandel at Christmas a few months earlier, our living room glowing from candlelight, we rationally and peacefully decided to keep this home for a bit longer, maybe a year. With so much change already encountered, we wanted to keep something the same, but it wasn't meant to be. For the next few weeks, life morphed into a chaotic stream of searching for listings, measuring furniture, scheduling appointments for showings, and occasionally crying in the bathroom. We didn't choose this. Nothing else mattered but finding our new home, so I scaled back as much as I could. The only thing I absolutely *had* to do was finish the final edits of my cookbook, but new blog posts and planning an online course would have to wait, carefully stored away.

We found a new condo only a mile away and booked a mover. We sold the sectional where I spent afternoons nursing Henry because it wouldn't fit in our new living room. I was heartbroken over that couch for months. I often resisted the urge to open my laptop instead of packing up my kitchen. Before any of this happened, and probably during the same conversation when we decided not to leave our condo yet, I chose a word for the year: *purpose*. My hope was to become closer to finding where I fit in the world and defining more clearly the kind of work to pursue. I wanted to feel rooted, confident, and pointed in the right direction, yet the year was turning into perpetual, infinite liminal space.

Not only were we setting up a new home, but I also felt an urge to leave my job. Without listing the irrelevant details, I'll simply divulge that during my interview process I wasn't privy to the organization's inner workings, and it quickly became a place

I no longer wished to be. I stayed because I got pregnant, something that did not come easily, and wanted to take a paid maternity leave. During those months I knew it was time to move on, but I didn't know what to do next.

I considered freelancing, something I'd watched friends do over the years but didn't feel prepared for. In my downtime, I brainstormed what I might do and who I might help. I pitched a few potential clients and designed a new website for myself that I ultimately never published. On my birthday I recorded an application video for a position and emailed it in. I was doing the opposite of waiting and listening. I didn't want wisdom just then, I wanted a new source of income. The urgency, while palpable, didn't last.

That summer I was inspired to finish developing the online course I'd been itching to create. Although I welcomed a few dozen writers into the group, it wasn't enough to support myself. I reluctantly began applying to jobs again, thirteen in total, when a recruiter emailed me out of the blue one morning, explaining the details of a position I knew I was perfect for. This had never happened in my entire career. My word for the year—*purpose*—rose up like a beacon, and a few weeks later I parked my car in a new lot, walked into the lobby, and gratefully entered a new season.

This time, I gave myself space. I said calmly and matter-of-factly to my creativity: *You just wait. Give me two weeks, then we'll meet again.* The weekend before my first day of work, I steamed a few shirts, scheduled my upcoming newsletters, and closed the drafts of my blog posts. I intentionally did nothing but go to work and come home, adjust to a new position and new routines. But I kept a few creative rhythms alive, like reading on my lunch break. My younger self would have never thought to do this. When you're transitioning, stay in writing's orbit a little, because it'll all stir up eventually.

-*Rituals & Routines*-

CHOOSE A WORD OF THE YEAR

December 31st always feels like its own sanctuary of liminal space, a day when the old year closes like a book before the new year unfurls. This brief window is an ideal time to designate a word to inform your year, a practice I've adopted to help serve as a guide for what's to come, unknown as it might be. It's less about to-do lists and more about how you want to feel as the year progresses.

SET AN INTENTION. Even if you're eager to choose a word, it's not a process to rush. The best approach is to nudge your subconscious to start sorting this out for you sometime in October or November. It might take a week or a month. Give yourself time to mull it over. Reflect on the current year and as far ahead as you can see, what the new year might bring.

How do you want to feel?

What do you need more of in your life?

What do you need less of?

CONSIDER THE CURRENT YEAR IN BOTH YOUR WRITING LIFE AND YOUR PERSONAL LIFE. What was missing? What was hard, what came easily? A word might surface and you know in your heart it's the right one. But if several emerge, collect them and wait. Think and ponder some more, and if you'd like, talk it over with a close friend, significant other, or your writing group.

ONCE YOU COMMIT TO A WORD, EMBODY IT. Don't concern yourself with making the wrong choice. The beauty of a single word is it can manifest in different ways throughout the year. For example, the year my son was born, I chose the word *open*, which ended up applying to both my birth experience, as my body needed to open for him to be born, and also being open-minded about new job possibilities. Don't overthink it, just be aware of the word and enjoy seeing how it shapes your year.

Except, It's Not Really Over

Unfortunately, a bout of liminal space in no way protects us from subsequent seasons. This is my way of telling you, I'm here again. At first it was just an occasional week or two, like when Andrew went to San Francisco for a conference. I didn't write that week, mostly because by the time I got home from work, made dinner, bathed Henry, and tucked him into bed, I was ready for bed myself. Then Andrew flew home, life normalized, and my back didn't hurt as much from bending over the tub to reach Henry's slender shoulders with my soapy hands.

But we're enduring another liminal space together, and it's more chronic than acute, so I'm unsure how long we'll be here. It started over the holidays, as these shifts tend to do. I should probably vow not to make any decisions in December by candlelight, wine in hand. Andrew started considering the next step in his career, which could mean leaving the company he's called home for nearly five years. We don't know if we'll stay in Los Angeles or move out of state, even out of the country. There are more questions than answers, and we've been talking about all the potential scenarios and how we feel about them. I also devote an obscene amount of time browsing listings on realtor.com and daydreaming about the future.

During that fateful conversation we decided the best thing to do was take it slow. This was to be a year of research and contemplating what's to come, especially since I had a book to write and we didn't want to feel rushed. But Andrew has just been recruited for a job right here in L.A., on the other side of town, where we have some friends with an avocado tree in their backyard. We could plant some roots, and Henry could start elementary school.

So we're imagining our new life. One phone interview has turned into another, which has turned into a six-hour in-person interview. It feels fast but right, like everything we've been wanting has been served up, so we're seizing it. We're craving change. Last weekend we visited a park and drove through a few neighborhoods. We told our parents. My mom, a real estate agent, sent me the contact information for her lender so we can get approved for a mortgage. Now we wait. Now I write. Now I remember how I survived all The Seasons of Liminal Space that have come before.

Crossing the Threshold

This isn't the sentence I was expecting to write, but they offered the job to someone else. Our dream, so quickly yet perfectly formed, has dissolved in an instant and we must start again, resigned to wade through liminal space a while longer. Life is strange. I'm filled with creative energy, yet I don't know where I'll live next year, if we'll stay or go. There is uncertainty and excitement and hesitation. So I'm writing and reading my way through it. And breathing on my mat and soaking in salt baths and waiting for life to unfold around me. Here are three things that are helping: not thinking about it, making my yoga class intention to accept what is, and writing to you.

It's my birthday, and with the news still fresh, both Andrew and I take the day off and drive to the Getty Villa, high on a hill and home to ancient sculptures, carved in stone. We stand in front of busts: Head of a Man, Head of a Woman. A nose obscured, a limb removed, damaged but still standing. There's one face, an emperor, and I wonder about him. This medium—preservation through stone—tells a story. It may be his likeness, or we might be gazing into the face he wanted to be remembered by, or how the artist chose to interpret his features. Aren't we always poised to discern what's true and what isn't? Every day—on Instagram, on the pages of our journal, in text messages and emails—we make an impression of our own design. The two of us curl up on a bench overlooking the Pacific. The sky is gray and the water is hazy, like we're looking through a steamy window. We know the vastness is there but can barely make out the surface of the water. We decide to take comfort in the uncertainty, to write a new story, and to find contentment in the infinite ocean of not knowing. At least, we want to try to do what the poet Rainer Maria Rilke suggested, to love the questions themselves and to live them.

The word *liminal* comes from the Latin word *limens*, meaning threshold. We are at the start of something new, you and I, about to break through the surface and emerge like that brave little seed, alone in the darkness yet somehow transformed, reaching for sun. Some days this is all we can count on, and for now, it must be enough.

–8–

The Season of
Visibility

The act of writing is a solitary one, but occasionally we must step out of the shadows. When it's time to journey to the outside world—share our work, connect with readers, or use social media—take the reins to support your calling.

What kills a soul? Exhaustion, secret
keeping, image management.
And what brings a soul back from the
dead? Honesty, connection, grace.
—SHAUNA NIEQUIST

Finding Wings

The year my parents brought home a boxy Apple II computer, I played "Oregon Trail" after school and typed up short stories on the green-lit screen. Underneath each title, a pseudonym: *By Samantha Douglas*, a name I felt sounded like a mature writer well beyond her first decade. The same day I went looking for my old pink notebook, about the time this book's first draft was blooming, I also unearthed archived files where some of my old stories had been kept for years. The poor writing I encountered wasn't a surprise, but I was alarmed to find my social security number printed on top of each page, under my address and phone number. Please don't do this.

Most of the stories that left home were returned. Occasionally I'd receive a kind note encouraging me to keep trying, which I did, believing the simple act of persistence would lead to publication eventually. I kept the routine throughout high school and college, which helped me practice the other side of the writer's life—sharing, waiting, and detaching from the work once it left my hands. Every few months I printed out the poems that felt finished, chose three that fit well together, then recorded their titles in a spreadsheet to be sure none were simultaneously submitted. Cover letters were polished, signed, and placed on top of the poems. I folded the bundle and slid it inside a gold paper pouch before walking to the post office with all of my poems, all of my heart, printed on the most economical ream of white paper I could find at Staples, ready to ship to literary magazines.

This was my first brush with The Season of Visibility, which arrives when it's time to step into bookstores, write blog posts, and record podcast interviews with our mouth up against a microphone. We're temporarily finished drafting, crossing out, changing pens, and telling ourselves we can't possibly say that, then saying it anyway. For so long, we're the only ones who know what's possible, what our soul whispers at any given moment. And then the moment comes to tell everyone about it, risk rejection slips, check in to conferences, and talk to strangers. There may be open-mic nights, empty bookstores, graduate school lectures, or a series of guest posts drawing attention to your story, all of which can feel at once magical and incredibly unnerving. Yet it's these slightly thorny spaces where we establish relationships with fellow writers and build trust with our readers. Growth is about the only thing that's guaranteed.

In the time between sending my short stories to magazines at age ten to sitting on panels during my first book tour at age thirty-five, I've learned that being bold with your stories and feeling at ease sharing your work is a slow progression. There are probably some naturally confident writers innately wired to thrive in public settings, but I don't know many of them. For the rest of us, we must resolve to inch forward, repeat things, and wade into slightly uncomfortable depths to embrace our voice off the page.

Do you feel like you're more composed on paper, and as soon as your mouth opens you lose all eloquence? Me too. The only thing that helps with this is practice. So if you're wondering whether or not you can be a writer who doesn't share her work with others, the answer is yes. But I believe regardless of scale—whether you have only a few dozen readers or ten thousand—there's someone out there who will benefit from reading the words only you can write. And that's reason enough to keep at it. Besides, after a certain moment, the words are no longer yours. The shift might occur when pages are printed, packages are sealed, or books are held for the first time. You've done your best with those sentences, and it's time to send them on. Remember this each time you affix a stamp. Let the words land where they may.

Flourishing in this season requires bravery, as well as some separation of ourselves from the page. We'll be called on to tell our stories repeatedly, and to believe in ourselves publicly. All the while, we must remember to tend to our inner world (take a page from The Season of Listening to Your Body) while navigating the outer world. From poetry readings to teaching to introducing yourself to another writer you admire (or just the person sitting next to you at an event), if you're visible, you're vulnerable. A piece may be dismantled by well-meaning workshop participants. That writer who said she'd email you never does. Your story is in the wild, known. But most things worth doing are at times perilous—having a child, saying vows, leaving home, waking up every day, and writing. There's risk in it all.

Hello, My Name Is . . .

By my late twenties, I realized I needed to establish my own human resources department. When I worked in philanthropy, I attended a couple of conferences each year and took trainings on everything from brochure design to analyzing financial audits. But writers have no such support. No one will voluntarily research MFA programs, ask us where we'd like to be in five years, or book our flight to a writing retreat. These tasks fall to us, so I like to take inspiration from the growth mind-set I exercised for so many years working for foundations, nonprofits, and food start-ups—become your own director of HR and seek out ways to cultivate your writing life.

Conferences are a popular place for writers to gather. Some events are more intimate, while others are overwhelmingly large, with sessions from morning to night. If the mere thought of interacting with so many strangers feels like too much, enlist a friend to attend. Also remember, these events are wonderful places to gather information and discover inspiration outside your daily routine. There's usually something for everyone—you can sit in the audience and take notes. You can meet with agents and pitch your book idea, if you want. You can attend the mixers or lunches. But if you prefer to melt into the crowd, you can do that too. Personally, I've always been nervous raising my hand in situations like this. Heads turn to look at me, and my comment never sounds as good as it did in my head moments earlier. If you share the same concern, simply listen. And here's my secret to surviving small talk: ask questions. Ask where they're from, what they write, or what brought them to the event. More often than not, you'll discover a common ground.

Prepare to be a bit more exposed if you attend a workshop, because you'll share your work in progress and get feedback from writers you've never met before. Retreats are more of a hybrid experience, typically in smaller groups where you get to know fellow writers over a weekend. You connect quickly and deeply, and while the days are restorative and refreshing, some are equally challenging. Whether you stay close to home or fly across the country, opportunities abound. Take a one-day workshop in town or sign up for a semester-long class at a local university. No matter what you do—whether you escape for a few hours or a few days—it will do your writer's heart some good. And a willingness to be visible might even shake you out of a rut. (See The Season of Retreating for a more in-depth look.)

-Rituals & Routines-

EXPLORE PROFESSIONAL DEVELOPMENT

When you set intentions, resolutions, or dreams for the year ahead, include your writing life in the conversation too. Set aside an hour to brainstorm a few of the things you'd like to do and research opportunities that might suit you.

> Arrange for a night or two away from home to write
> Join a local writing group
> Attend a conference or retreat
> Take an online course
> Grab a friend and go to poetry readings
> Hire an editor to help polish an essay
> Get a library card (and use it)

> Publish an author website

> Start a blog

> Subscribe to new literary magazines

> Pick an author and read every book they've written

Next, add whatever you decide to pursue to the calendar and submit your time-off request, if needed. Then you can start anticipating taking better care of the writer in you.

Nurture Your Readers

Making space to write while also developing a readership is a delicate balance, and choosing where to direct your energy is paramount. Of course, you should spend most of your time writing. But it's also good to build a community. After all, who will buy your book, come hear you read, or sign up for your workshop? For a writer embarking on a Season of Visibility, these questions need answering.

There are many ways to do this, and entire books have been written about the art of audience building, but here's what feels authentic to me. One of the most important things I've done for my writing life has been inviting others into it. I do this by sending a weekly newsletter to encourage fellow writers and creatives who are alongside me for the journey. The early days were terribly inconsistent. Some weeks I sent two notes, or it was every three weeks, or every other week. I couldn't reliably tell anyone when they might hear from me, and waiting for inspiration to strike was my only strategy.

After a few months I got serious and made a schedule: the first day of every month. This was my routine for a year, during a season when my work life was particularly demanding, but I eventually felt ready to alter the regularity to once per week. After my first hundred subscribers signed up, I sent personal notes to each person, thanking them for allowing me into their inbox. No matter what, consistency is more important than frequency. Whether you're writing each Tuesday or every three weeks, the person on the other end will appreciate knowing what to expect. And what exactly can they expect? It's up to you and based on the kind of writer you are.

A novelist might share about character development or send mini book reviews, someone who blogs about being an empty nester might provide tips for moving through this period of life, and a poet might reveal new poems-in-progress. I send insights from my writing life, including lessons I'm learning, struggles I'm facing, quotes from books I'm reading. Just remember that a newsletter is less about you and more about your readers. They'll sign up because what you have to offer meets a need in their life, whether it's inspirational or practical. They'll also unsubscribe, but don't wince when someone says goodbye—focus on the people who remain.

Gathering names for this budding newsletter will require an online home. Blogging is a wonderful way not only to practice the craft and hone your voice but also to provide space for others to cluster around a shared interest. Once they read a few posts and get to know you a bit, you can invite them to join you more intimately by sharing their email address.

Your newsletter is a tool. Yes, it will satisfy publishers who like to know who will be buying your book. But more important, the acts of blogging and sending a newsletter—talking to people on a regular basis—build relationships and foster trust. At times it's a slow process, but I prefer it that way.

As for social media, if you spend any time researching this vast topic, you'll find many *shoulds* are mentioned. A writer should have a Facebook page. A writer should post to Instagram twice a day and bare her soul. A writer should create Pinterest graphics and embed them in her blog. A writer should send newsletters every Tuesday morning. But my philosophy only requires an answer to one simple question: does this feel good to me?

Being a successful writer doesn't mean having an active presence on every site. Using multiple platforms will only drain your energy for the real work to be done, so be selective and adopt the medium that feels fun and energizing. This approach will help you focus more on serving others than on amassing likes or comments and will help preserve your boundaries too.

Keep Towels in the Car, and Other Lessons from Book Tour

Two days after *Eat This Poem* was published, I held my first event at Vroman's Bookstore in Pasadena. To prepare I started with my hair, treating myself to a blowout that gave me effortless-looking waves. I moved on to the nail salon for a manicure and pedicure in a soft pink hue. Nothing flashy, but when I looked down at my hands, I wanted them to look cared for. At home I picked out a cashmere sweater and nude leather loafers. Then I started talking to myself. It's a tool I picked up in college, when I was trained in public speaking while working for the freshmen orientation program.

For two summers I led groups of students through the choppy waters of signing up for their first classes, hosted tours (while walking backward), and gave academic-requirement presentations to groups of two hundred anxious parents. But before any of this happened, our team spent months preparing. In winter we memorized the undergraduate courses, practiced our presentations, and anticipated questions. If we didn't know the answer, we were trained to say, "I don't know, but I'll find out and get back to you." We also learned tricks like pacing back and forth on stage to keep an audience's interest or holding a small token in our pocket, like a paper clip, to rub with our finger and absorb nervous energy. Another thing we learned: No one is out to make you stumble. If they're in the audience, they're interested, not malicious. I can't tell you how much calmer this makes me, even now.

Being prepared was always the key to our program's success, and I've upheld a similar philosophy in my writing life. Before a podcast interview, bookstore reading, or even a phone call with my editor, I practice out loud. It doesn't eliminate nerves, but it helps me feel more at ease. If you're sharing your work in any capacity—from a reading of unpublished poems to a signing for your third book—you're undergoing the process of becoming a more authentic version of yourself.

That afternoon before my book signing, I left three hours early to avoid rush-hour traffic, and conversations with myself continued across town. I turned down the jazz station and reviewed the questions my friend and event cohost, Amelia, emailed me the week before, recalling which stories I wanted to tell and the comments I'd make about each poem before reading it. I parked underneath a shady tree in the lot behind the bookstore, then walked inside and meandered through the aisles as my stomach swirled with butterflies, blended with the sheer pleasure of seeing a stack of my books at the bottom of the staircase. I stood at the back of the event space for a moment, wondering about the chairs. I counted at least forty, which was far more people than I hoped to recruit, but pushed the thought from my mind and headed down the street for a cup of tea.

A gust of wind blew newspaper pages in front of me as I strolled, but before I kicked them away I recognized the face on the cover of *Pasadena Weekly*. I'd done a phone interview a few weeks earlier but didn't realize my book jacket photo would be printed in color on the front page. There I was, smiling with long, bouncy curls around my face, leaning into a pillow on the couch with a favorite mug in my hand. We had a photographer come by to take some newborn portraits six weeks after Henry was born, and I decided since I swiped on a coat of lipstick, I should take some new headshots. I crouched down to pick up a few copies of the paper, stuffed them into my purse, and kept bounding down the sidewalk.

If you're hoping to distract yourself before an event starts, it might prove difficult. I brought a book but read for only a few minutes before reopening the folded page of questions, the ones I knew well enough by now, and told myself a version of what I'd been repeating all day: *You wrote a book, and tonight you get to celebrate. Stay present.*

Walking back to the bookstore, I transferred the half-empty tea cup from my left hand to my right and shifted my shoulder in the process. Instead of gracefully tossing the cup into the trash can, I fumbled. The lid wasn't tightly secured, and I spilled cold chamomile all over myself. Thankfully, my sweater was a dark navy and, also thankfully, I had an old towel rolled in the trunk of my car to blot some of the dampness away. This kind of thing can happen, so watch your movements closely, and bring towels, napkins, or a change of shirt, just in case.

And about that sweater, covered in tea. Remember that no one cares about what you're wearing. It doesn't matter if you're donning a dress, a blazer, pointed flats, or boots. There could be an exception if you're attending a formal dinner or benefit, but the majority of events in bookstores, historical societies, stages on college campuses, or private homes don't require anything but dressing in a way that makes you feel as comfortable as possible.

A few months earlier I met some friends for dinner. They both had books out already, and when I asked for event tips, one of them quickly mentioned the power outfit, admitting she bought a few extra pieces before heading out on the road. Elizabeth Suzann is a favorite brand of mine, and the designer and founder Liz Pape once wrote a blog post about all the ways clothing can serve us, such as eliminating distraction, quieting insecurity, and amplifying confidence. This is not about vanity but comfort. When you're in a situation that makes you feel vulnerable, feeling empowered by the clothes that drape your body can help you project your warmth and energy to the person sitting in the back row. So if you're preparing to attend a conference, a book signing, or any other public event, consider your closet.

A final note on preparation: bring snacks. Almonds, homemade muffins, packets of maple-sweetened peanut butter, or whatever else you like. Some events cut into regular meal times, and you don't want to worry about your stomach rumbling while you're reading a passage from your book.

-Rituals & Routines-

TALK TO YOURSELF

Before an interview, book signing, or panel, make sure to prepare. Don't be shy about talking to yourself when you practice!

ANTICIPATE COMMON QUESTIONS. One of the fears I still have about public speaking is not knowing what someone will ask ahead of time. Thinking on my feet always makes me more nervous than being armed with a list of talking points, but you can ease some of the concern simply by putting yourself in your audience's shoes.

If you've written a memoir, someone might ask what your family thought, or what you learned in the course of writing the book. For fiction, they'll want to know how you came up with the idea, who your favorite character is, if any part of the story is autobiographical, or how you conducted research. There could be interest in your writing process, as well as general themes in the book.

For podcasts or media interviews, ask for a list of questions ahead of time. What you say to yourself won't necessarily come out rehearsed in the moment, but preparedness will help you reign in answers that might go off on tangents, deliver a succinct elevator pitch, and be less likely to forget something important you want to convey.

READ ALOUD. Before an event, review sections of your book to become more at ease with your inflections, and time yourself to be sure you're staying within the allotment you've been given.

MAKE A MANTRA. There'll be a moment in the subway ride over, or in your seat about to go on stage, when you might wonder how you got there, what you're doing facing an audience instead of sitting in one, or if what you have to say is worthy of hearing. When this happens to me, I always take a moment to say some version of the following to myself: *Nicole, you have an amazing opportunity today. You've been invited to talk about your book, share your story, and continue walking down the writer's path. Just be yourself.* It helps every time.

REMEMBER YOUR BREATH. For anxiety, the technique of alternate-nostril breathing can help your nervous system calm down. You can also try a gentle tapping technique, taking your index and middle fingers and gently tapping them over your heart for a few moments.

What We're Really Selling

When Henry was a few months old, I started going to the farmers' market alone on Saturday mornings because it was faster than loading him in the car and navigating the stalls with a stroller. One weekend a musician strummed his guitar while the rest of us picked up fruit and potatoes. I liked his sound, so I stuffed a ten-dollar bill into his jar and picked up a CD. I might not have done this before I'd written a book, but now I was on the other side, with something to share and to sell, and I knew what it felt like to have to find ways to accomplish both of those goals without feeling itchy all over. He had a trick, though—play two songs, thank everyone for listening, then mention his album. It was all very conversational, but he wasn't shy about letting us know how we could support him.

I drove home thinking about his approach, and how it might apply to writers. It's easy to assume everyone is tired of hearing our story, but the way social media and shifting algorithms work these days, it's unlikely everyone who follows you on every social platform will see your caption. Repeating it is one of our jobs. Plus, maybe you've heard the marketing adage that someone must be exposed to a message at least seven times before they're ready to take action.

You don't need to set up shop at a farmers' market to sell your book. (Although if you wrote a cookbook, this might be smart.) There are podcasts and guests posts and social media giveaways and live television segments. Don't underestimate your family and friends either. It's possible they'll be some of your most enthusiastic supporters and tell everyone they know about the book. So let's reframe self-promotion. It's not about selling something but about helping someone. We meet readers where they are. What we have to offer is perspective, experience, hope, inspiration. You're simply putting a book in the hands and hearts of readers who can benefit from your message.

The Energy in the Room

At the Pasadena event—the one where I spilled tea on myself—there were ten people in the audience. I counted them from my director's chair: My mom and two of her friends from aqua aerobics, my friend Amy who lived nearby, and Amelia's husband. The other five were patrons already shopping at the bookstore who decided to sit in after seeing the event sign. I was grateful to the unknown force that propelled them to slip into the seats.

It was seven o'clock on a Thursday night in Los Angeles, and Angelenos don't drive to the other side of town at rush hour. I knew this in my bones and could have sunk into my chair but decided to show up instead. I gave all my energy to those sitting in front of me, and we carried on talking about food memories and poetry, as if the room were full, as if we didn't notice the gaps between rows.

Afterward, I signed extra store copies, took pictures for my mom to share on Facebook, and profusely thanked the event coordinator. Then I walked to my car, turned on the headlights, and drove home. I called Andrew as soon as I pulled out of the parking lot. "You know what," I said, "I made all this fuss. I did my hair and nails, took the day off from work, and it was over in less than an hour." Under the street lamps of Colorado Boulevard, I realized this was only the beginning. It was the event to help shift my mind into event mode, to remind me I could do it and find joy in depleting my coveted introvert energy for a night. Like two days earlier when my book was finally published, this evening also turned into a "secret anniversar[y] of the heart," as the poet Henry Wadsworth Longfellow so beautifully wrote.

Sometimes The Season of Visibility isn't only about shaking hands or taking over an Instagram feed, but about connecting with yourself too—seeing what you're made of, what you're capable of, and the heartwarming reward of watching others discover and enjoy your work. But the season is fleeting, and its glow fades like a tan you proudly wore for a few weeks after your tropical vacation. The next poem or story or blog post won't write itself. Eventually you must return to the page. Besides, the book isn't the end. Neither is the op-ed or the TED talk. These opportunities to share our story more widely are only the beginning.

And yes, you might be mistaken for another, more famous writer and watch readers leave disappointed when they learn you, an unknown first-time author, are the three o'clock slot and they arrived on the wrong day. You might discover your reading will take place in a courtyard, in the hot sun, with shoppers passing by. You might sweat more profusely than usual. You might feel all the energy you were holding redistribute throughout your body as soon as you return to your seat or leave the building, like you're in desperate need of a massage. You might laugh and enjoy yourself. You might even cry after reading an email where someone said you inspired them. (All of these things have happened to me.)

At Thanksgiving last year my mother-in-law mentioned how amazing it is that preparing the meal takes hours, most of a day even, yet is devoured so quickly. All the more reason to love the process, I thought. Milestones are motivating, and there's great pleasure in seeing your words make their way in the world. But if the writing itself and the deeper discovery of yourself along the way aren't enough, then those milestones will never sustain you. If the unfinished words aren't beautiful today, then publishing a poem in a prestigious literary journal tomorrow won't be enough either. Because the next day some of the acclaim will fade, and you'll wake up on the same side of the bed as you always do, perform all the mundane tasks life requires, stirring sugar into coffee or wiping down the mirrors or the toilet seat or taking the dog for a walk. In between, the words beckon and the page will be blank, until it isn't.

-9-

The Season of
Retreating

As important as it is to engage, writers must also
retreat. Leaving the house, disconnecting from your
online home, and tuning out the noise of everything
you think you should be doing can restore your
spirit and reconnect you to the craft.

To hear ourselves, we sometimes
have to flee ourselves,
diving into silence until we're uncomfortably
alone with the noise within.

—MEGHAN O'ROURKE

An Early Flight

My aisle seat, 3C, has extra leg room in exchange for wedging my purse into the overhead bin. I arrange a folder of essays, a magazine, and a black pen on my lap while the couple next to me orders cocktails: vodka and tomato juice for him, champagne and orange juice for her. Not long into the flight, my pen choice proves disastrous—it leaks, leaves blotches on the page, and streaks my left index finger. Actually, both my hands have smudges. Is it an omen that I shouldn't have come? *No, no,* I tell myself. *You need this. You deserve this. You've come to meet other people who write, who are in the trenches like you. You've come to put one word in front of the other, and you will.* I give up on underlining and taking notes and slip the pen onto the floor, then unbuckle my seat belt and walk to the lavatory to wash my hands. The ink fades with two scrubbings, but traces remain.

After seven hours traveling by car, plane, bus, ferry, and another car, I arrive on Whidbey Island, off the coast of Seattle. I've come for refuge, to explore tough topics wholeheartedly, and to learn from twenty other writers about what it means to face the page with bravery. From my hotel balcony, pointed tips of evergreens form an uneven horizon across to Camano Island. I gaze into the water. It's high tide, and two ducks float, weightless things, like my son's plastic bath toys. I wonder if they are cold or hungry.

The entire body of water quivers and moves left, away from the sun, away from me. Nothing recedes. It's nearly spring, and I'm here to do what's elusive on most Tuesday mornings, when

I'm packing Henry's lunch box and dropping him off at preschool or sitting in a work meeting: to withdraw, to write, to rest. To leave behind chores, all that remains unfinished, and go within.

Although I've trained myself to seize margins as brief as five minutes to write, I'm unsure how I'll manage with two full days to myself. If I'll be capable of focusing. I first unpack my toothbrush and chunky sweaters and set Joan Didion's *Slouching Towards Bethlehem* on the long wooden entry table. I slip off my sneakers, spread my toes for the first time today, and reach my arms to the ceiling before zipping my suitcase, the one my dog sniffed before I rolled it out the door, knowing what it meant to see me pull it away from her. Tangled in my heart, a recurring tension—I want to leave home yet still want to feel at home. So I've traveled to the edge, looking out over a body of water, which is always a comforting posture. Except when I close the glass door behind me and plug my phone charger into the wall, I realize the solitude I craved will force me to address stories I've been reluctant to share. A blanket may drape my shoulders, but it can't protect me from the necessary silence and turning my ear to those dark, interior spaces.

Making Arrangements

There are always reasons not to go, especially because before you can immerse yourself in The Season of Retreating, however brief, there are details to tend to, meals to freeze, meetings to run, birthday parties to RSVP to, cars to wash. Daily tasks will always beckon. You may need to arrange extra childcare or modify carpool schedules. I can't deny that preparations must be made, which sometimes makes the very nature of retreating seem all the more challenging. There's also the expense, which can be economical or extravagant, depending on your budget.

If you're like me, you may appreciate the art of list making. I leave my husband notes for what to pick up at the grocery store, a list of meals to make with the ingredients. I open the refrigerator and freezer and point to the yogurt carton or the icy loaves of grain bread, already sliced for sandwiches. We talk about the schedule for the days I'll be gone.

When I travel, I'm interested in bringing the least amount of belongings, so for an item of clothing to be considered, it must be able to be worn more than once. Don't forget socks, which are valuable even if you only wear them at night while reading a book in bed. And whether it's an overnight stay in a hotel across town or a longer stretch of time a few states over, there are many ways to create this experience for yourself.

An official writing retreat ensures you'll meet other writers, work within a loose structure or curriculum before being set free for hours of writing time. You can also arrange your own retreat by driving to a B&B outside the city or booking a hotel in a neighborhood across town. If staying close by feels unsuitable for a true escape, take a moment and recall everything that happens from the time you wake up in the morning to the time your head rests on the pillow at night. Tasks like making the bed, preparing a Powerpoint presentation, sending emails, walking your dog, picking up your kids from school, making dinner, dusting—every domestic rhythm dissolves when you retreat. Time will feel more expansive, more drawn out, more tangible. You might not know what to do with yourself for three whole hours, laptop snug on your thighs. Even in a town you've lived in for years, it will feel luxurious to get ready so quickly, with only yourself to tend to and nowhere to be.

You can enjoy a leisurely lunch or a glass of wine. You can go to bed early and wake up late. You can go with a friend, sharing a room to make it more affordable, or stay separately but meet for meals. You can hold each other accountable and split the gas bill. You can spend one night away every two months, or one week away every year, or something in between. You can attend a retreat in your genre, or at a specific point in your writing process that might help you get unstuck. How you design the experience, how you get there, how far you travel, or how long you stay is not the most important thing. What matters is recognizing the feeling in your body of leaving your life behind and having nothing expected of you but to meet yourself on the page and see what you have to say.

-Rituals & Routines-

DESIGN YOUR RETREAT

One of the most important things to do before a retreat is know what you need from it. It's not enough to book a hotel and hope it goes well. The more intentional you are about what you hope to gain from a retreat, which may differ year to year, the greater chance you have of returning home truly refreshed. By definition a retreat is an act of withdrawal. We all need the opportunity to seclude ourselves, but the walls that hold us and the locations we look to may be vastly different.

To better determine what sort of retreat will work for you, ask yourself:

What's your budget?

How many days can you accommodate being gone?

Do you envision being alone or with other writers?

Would you prefer some structured activities and discussions, or is complete flexibility more appealing?

Are you looking for feedback on a work in progress or hoping to make headway on a draft?

Here are some other considerations to keep in mind.

ECONOMICS AND LOGISTICS. Setting a budget is the least exciting aspect of a retreat, but it will save you from exploring possibilities beyond your reach. Budget applies to money, of course, but also to time: how many nights can you arrange? Both conversations may require a partner, especially if they'll be helping with childcare, or your supervisor, to be sure work is covered in your absence. Once you're clear on how much you can spend and how many nights you can spare, the fun begins. First, the matter of your writing:

What are you hoping to draft or complete—a series of poems, a book proposal, the outline of your novel, or two chapters from your memoir?

Which stage of the writing process are you in? Are you staring down a blank page, are you transcribing old journal entries and notebook drafts to digital pages, or will you have a stack of printed pages in tow, ready for revision? Are you looking for instructors and fellow writers to provide inspiration, or are you in need of utter solitude, or a combination?

COMFORT. Do minimalist accommodations suit, or do you prefer a jetted jacuzzi tub and plush bathrobes? Dream up some of the amenities you'd enjoy—like spa treatments or being walking distance to good restaurants. Or would you rather rent a small apartment to make some of your own meals and brew coffee first thing in the morning? I once heard of a writer who took a solo cruise, staying onboard to finish her first draft instead of exploring the ports. No one ever said a writing retreat had to stay on dry land.

LOCATIONS. Where do you feel most at home in the world—on a mountain, near the ocean, anywhere under a palm tree, or in a bustling downtown city? Think of where you'd most like to be, or where you have friends to visit, then go forth and design your retreat and research opportunities. Book it, circle dates on the calendar, and carry with you the knowledge that in a few weeks or a few months, words will be waiting for you there.

If you live alone or you don't have children, it's easy enough to plan a writing retreat for yourself at home. Set aside a weekend, make a pitcher of iced tea or cold brew, and set a timer to go off every forty-five minutes so you can stretch a bit or take a quick walk outside. If you're prone to distracting yourself with vacuuming or cake baking, research a new coffee shop to try. Take yourself out to lunch or buy a new candle—just a little something to make the days feel extra special.

Withdrawing from Social Media

My first cell phone was kept in the console of my Nissan 280ZX for emergencies. More often I used it to let my parents know when I drove from one friend's house to another on Friday night, or if we planned a late-night run to In-N-Out. Texting, video calls, and browsing the internet wasn't contained in the palm of my hand. It was only a phone, a large, heavy one at that. Now our devices are smart, perhaps too smart. They've also grown into indispensable tools. My phone is always with me, standing in for a notebook on many occasions, capturing ideas and lines and a few sentences here and there. Early drafts of this book were written, in part, on my phone.

We're reliant on technology to build relationships, find readers, and expand our reach. I count social media as a catalyst for helping nurture some of my earliest relationships with fellow bloggers. Yet social media does the one thing writers need to protect themselves from at all cost: it often rings so loud it prevents us from hearing our own voice and believing in what it has to offer. We've all been caught up in the swell of social media, like being washed out to sea, not strong enough to pull our bodies back to shore. Whenever I find myself floating in a vast ocean of aimless scrolling, I know it's time to retreat and to reconsider my relationship to the digital world.

I don't believe the solution is to abandon these tools entirely. It's unlikely cell phones will become obsolete. If anything, they'll become more integrated in our lives, conceivably to great bene-fit, but we should take care to be mindful, deliberately retreat on occasion, so we can focus on making more space for creative endeavors, determine what's been harming our spirits, what's been enhancing it, and make adjustments so these platforms support us, not stifle us.

EMBARK ON A SOCIAL-MEDIA CLEANSE

Twice a year, in the summer and around the holidays, I do a social-media cleanse. Naturally, you can adapt it as you wish. I hope you'll try it at least once, though, because you'll likely emerge with new discoveries about your relationship with social media and, ultimately, your creativity. The most obvious benefit, and the one I hear most frequently from others I've led through this, is more time to write. So if you're willing, set aside a few days or a week and give it a try.

Before you begin, decide what you want to take away from this experience. How many changes are you willing to make? What would you like to spend more time doing? Know that discomfort is inevitable but temporary. Like all great insights, they usually rise from a blockage or a fear—something we have to work through, not around.

STEP 1: JUMP IN. Faced with the prospect of a cold swimming pool, it's tempting to wade in slowly, but a quick jump acclimates us to the temperature more easily. When it comes to social media, it may take anywhere from one to three days (but at least twenty-four hours) to leave it behind—fully.

If you're easily tempted by your phone, create a new folder called

"Cleanse" or "Hide" and drag your social-media apps there. Make it as difficult as possible, with multiple keystrokes, to access it. Next, note all the places your phone resides. If you use your phone as an alarm, put your phone on the other side of the room, so you're less likely to scroll through a news feed first thing in the morning. Don't upload photos of your lunch or your kids or your vacation. Don't unlock your screen while sitting at a red light (which you shouldn't be doing any-way). And speaking of lights, if you're easily distracted by the blinking variety, the one that sends your brain into a frenzy alerting you to a new comment or like or email, mute everything and turn off notifica-tions. These micro-movements in the direction of a more peaceful relationship with social media will make an enormous difference and may end up being some policies you elect to keep indefinitely.

STEP 2: SCAN YOUR BODY AND YOUR MIND. Awareness creates a shift. As you move through the day (or days) notice the habits you've formed, how you naturally reach for your phone at your desk or in your back pocket, like a reflex, and what you feel like you're missing out on when you don't have access to social media at all hours of the day. Maybe you'll feel liberated. Notice that too, and write it in a journal, if you like. You're used to scanning your feed, but scan your body instead, and scan your thoughts. Take a short walk without your phone. Think about something you're writing and turn it over in your mind, around and around, like sucking on a caramel.

During this period, embrace the possibility of replacing social media with more creative opportunities. As writers we need to work in tandem with our subconscious, but it can't thrive when our brain is constantly distracted. On a recent flight I pulled *Delta Sky Magazine* from the seat pocket and discovered an interview with Lin-Manuel Miranda, who wrote the musical *Hamilton*. When asked how he finds time to create, his reply affirmed everything I've come to learn about my own writing process. "The good idea comes in the moment of rest. It comes in the shower. It comes when you're doodling or playing trains with your son. *Hamilton* forced me to double down on being awake to the inspirations of just living my life." We must wake up. We must stay present.

STEP 3: SET NEW BOUNDARIES. The morning keynote speaker at a conference I attended years ago was the author Charles Duhigg, who wrote a book called *The Power of Habit*. He emphasized thinking about a habit that scares you, like your reliance on social media, and shared what he called the habit loop, consisting of a cue, a routine, and a reward.

You can reframe this in terms of what you want to remove, such as eliminating countless minutes scrolling through your Facebook feed before bed. The cue might start after getting home from work, when you plug your phone into a charger in the living room and leave it there overnight. The routine could feel treacherous at first and take a few days to warm up to. If you're motivated by rewards, treat yourself to a new book or a pedicure at the end of the week if you're successful.

As you prepare to introduce social media back into your routine, instill some new boundaries based on your experience with the habit loop.

> What did you miss?
> What can you let go of?

> Did you try anything new with your schedule that felt like a welcome change?
> What do you see yourself sticking with?
> Where did your energy peak during the day?

Here are some healthier boundaries from my own life, as well as from fellow writers who have undertaken the cleanse.

> Buy an alarm clock
> Read news in the afternoon, not first thing in the morning
> After getting to work, leave your phone in your purse for an hour or two
> No screen time after dinner
> Keep social-media apps in a separate folder, not on the home screen
> Update settings for groups you're a part of or pages you follow, so you're not notified of every single post
> Reduce the number of people you follow on Instagram
> Only check Twitter if someone mentions you directly

Other Ways to Find Refuge

Brief getaways aren't the only way to support a writing practice or to reduce our reliance on social media. There are other options, such as studying abroad. When I spent a semester in London, part of our assignments in a literature seminar involved walking in the footsteps of Virginia Woolf through Bloomsbury's gardens and visiting the former home of Charles Dickens. I believe in the power of a room, a desk, a space to feel at home with our work, but sometimes exploring is in order. Wherever you land, another country might offer a new perspective and ignite some inspiration not accessible at home.

Holidays provide another opportunity to cultivate a with-drawing mind-set. Writers may fall into one of two camps during these periods. Some are energized by the time off and vow to write even more than usual, while others feel overwhelmed with all the merriment activities and fear writing will pull them away from spending time with family and enjoying the season. As with all things, our choices come at cost, so ask yourself, *What am I willing to give up?* During the holidays I shift into the lessons gleaned from The Season of Liminal Space and try to consume more than create. I give myself space, a lot of it if necessary. It can be a natural time to retreat *from* writing, but if you do keep writing, adjust your expectations so you're not worried about deadlines and word counts during the festivities.

Finally, there's graduate school, which can serve as a more long-term retreat. A traditional program will be more immersive, requiring your life to relocate for two or three years. I chose a low-residency program with the flexibility to keep my California home base while tailoring course work to my interests, but I almost faltered after hauling my suitcase up a set of stairs, cheeks flushed, looking over the quad for the first time. The January snow was white and unmoving. There was no wind. Bare branches stood resolute. *Why have I come?* I wondered. How did I end up in a corner dormitory room during winter? I had two hours before my first session, followed by dinner in the basement cafeteria. What was I doing there? Retreating, I reminded myself. For eleven days, twice a year. Dedicating my days to writing. Giving myself a gift.

The residencies will afford an opportunity to establish new, temporary rhythms surrounding your writing life. I wasn't a parent yet, but I felt beholden to my job as a media researcher, which I continued in the early mornings before my workshops started. I sat bundled in layers at my desk, Googling how old heaters worked because I had never used one and mine shot out strong bursts of steam in the middle of the night. I never did get the heater to work properly, but there was also something exhilarating about the cold, like every sense in my body was sharper and like new words might follow. That's always one value of a retreat, graduate school or otherwise—the shock, emotionally or physically, awakening inspiration.

The Greatest Fear of All

It's our last morning on the island. I arrive at the breakfast room early and fill my plate with smoked salmon and herbed cheese, plus a mini quiche teetering on the rim. I'm waiting to meet with one of the instructors for our one-on-one session. Jess and I have only thirty minutes together so we talk quickly, bonding over our shared type-A tendencies and how we use yoga to help untangle creative knots. "Have you ever brought a notebook into class before?" she asks. I haven't but log the suggestion away and start babbling about *Wild Words*. "So, I'm writing a book about writing a book," I share. "It's a meditation on the writer's life, and I'm hoping to provide a new way for people to relate to their creativity, to see it more seasonally."

She recommends *This Is the Story of a Happy Marriage* by Ann Patchett, which I've recently started reading. "Ann does that a bit, moving back and forth between memories while talking about living the writer's life." I ask if it's possible for me to be a trustworthy narrator in the first person, writing as I go, and she assures me it is. With only a few minutes left, I move on to something I haven't stopped thinking about since last night. "I really struggled with the fear-naming exercise," I tell her. "Everything I wrote down was wrong. A few of the fears were close, but I knew the whole time that something was missing."

I'm afraid my life is boring.
I'm afraid of people misunderstanding me.
I'm afraid my memories feel bigger and more meaningful in
my mind than they really are.
I'm afraid I'm still so far from who I'm meant to be.

But then something unexpected happened. After closing our notebooks we all slipped back to our rooms to change for yoga. Mats overlapped in a room too small to contain us, but we still looked out over the water, overcome with the view. The instructor had the loudest lion's breath I'd ever heard—frightening and thrilling at once, as though he was letting loose a fire from deep inside his belly. A few minutes into class, he slowly recited a Marianne Williamson quote, one he believed in so strongly it was tattooed on his foot, words to stand on. "Our deepest fear is not that we are inadequate. Our deepest fear is that we are powerful beyond measure." In downward dog, head reaching toward my chest, my eyes welled with tears. *That's it*, I thought. This whole time I've been afraid of becoming the writer I've always imagined myself to be—no longer placing writing on the perimeter of my life, but being centered by it.

Before our time's up, I tell Jess about how my shoulders started shaking at the thought, how I often wonder what happens after what you've been dreaming of, arms outstretched, is finally realized. How do I move from reaching to receiving, and sit comfortably in gratitude after spending nearly two decades operating as though writing books was out of my grasp? These are the questions I'm taking home. Jess smiles, happy I'd experienced what she and the other instructors hoped—some breakthrough to move the work forward, move *me* forward. If it took three nights away from home to understand this fear more deeply, even if I hadn't written a single word while I was there, it would have been enough.

-*Rituals & Routines*-

TRUST THE JOURNEY

If long stretches of time pass between retreats, you might feel an urgency to squeeze out every benefit and imbue every moment with meaning. But a word of caution: don't put too much pressure on the experience. Doing so might lead to decision fatigue in the moment or berating yourself for taking a nap instead of writing. Trust that what you need to learn will arrive in its time and go from there.

Before your next retreat, write an intention in your journal before you leave and revisit it when you travel. Here's one I've set for myself in the past:

I'm retreating to deepen my writing and connect with myself. Permission to rest, read, or write as I feel led is granted. I promise to stay open, stay present, and be gentle with any emotions that surface, whether in my heart or on the page.

Home Again

"Hi, Henry! What'd you do today?" I ask, climbing into the seat next to him.

"I look for red airplanes. Maybe we see another one?"

"Oh, you were looking for airplanes in the sky?"

Andrew pushes the button to open the sunroof as we merge into the traffic circle at LAX.

"Mommy got on a plane and went to Seeee-attle." Henry announces.

As we drive home, I kiss his forehead and touch his leg. In the parking garage, Henry insists on helping me push my suitcase into the elevator, shuffling in his socks.

Once inside, I quickly eat dinner, saved in the refrigerator for me, while Andrew starts the bathwater. I unzip my bag and pull out a book, *The Tale of Peter Rabbit*, that I bought at Moonraker Books in Langley. After chatting with the owner about how she used to live in Southern California and I mentioned staying at the inn down the road, she dragged me to the sidewalk, left the store unattended, and marched me into her favorite restaurant on 1st Street—Latin-inspired tapas, seafood, pizza sold by the slice. "You'd never know these were here if you didn't step inside," she said.

Getting up from the couch, I swing my neck around hoping to loosen some of the stiffness, then turn on the kitchen faucet. Our roles resume. I scrub the dishes, hear Andrew ask Henry if he wants bubbles in the tub and which bath toy he'd like to play with tonight. I wash the plates, wonder what I'll make for dinner tomorrow, then pull out my clothes and start a load of laundry. I've been home less than an hour, and already I'm back to sorting, planning, and the rest of it. Everything wonderful around me, Mary Oliver always reminds.

What feels like an indulgence—a soaking tub, locally sourced meals, homemade granola at breakfast, yoga—is not. Without space, our ideas can't be finished. We're left with well-intentioned but incomplete sentences. Thoughts are not whole but scattered in pieces. Eventually we need a surge of momentum to see us through. Yes, we can always begin at home, and we do. We must. We will write in the margins, but there comes a moment, and you'll know when it is, that escape feels essential and imminent, like you'll somehow burst without a day or two to hear yourself think.

But there is still a strangeness in coming home. Although re-treating helps restore us, the energy doesn't always last. We return with souvenirs of more words written, but inevitably we'll fall into the very routines we ached to leave. Andrew sneaks out of Henry's bedroom and finds me typing, shares a new song Henry taught him. The interruptions have begun again. I'm back in it, but I'm changed, ever so slightly more open, bending toward the words like a flower drawn to sunlight.

-10-

The Season of
Finishing

The triumphant last sentence or final draft is cause for celebration, but it's only made possible by setting a strong foundation, staying disciplined, and being gracious with yourself along the way. I'd say this is where it all ends, but it might also be the start of something new.

Sometimes when you think you are done,
it is just the edge of beginning.

—NATALIE GOLDBERG

Writing in the Dark

Henry is asleep in his travel crib a few feet from our bed. It's three in the afternoon. The shades are drawn for his nap and my computer screen is on the dimmest setting. We're in Santa Barbara for a few days, passing some time during Henry's spring break from preschool, and while we've enjoyed picnics in wine country and running through the sand, I can't ignore the pull to get back, especially with the manuscript due soon. I've been going over one section for days, and inconveniently, an idea for sorting out the chapter arrived, almost fully formed, after cutting Henry's peanut butter and jelly sandwich into four triangular pieces. While we ate together, I spotted a thin pad of paper and a hotel pen shoved on the other side of the table. Knowing I'd forget my thought by the time we finished eating the last of the sweet potato chips, I frantically started writing.

Andrew coughs next to me, half asleep. This isn't the most ideal environment to continue writing a book. I can't see the keyboard, for one. I can't see the notes I scribbled on the flimsy pad a half an hour earlier. Andrew gets up to find a bag of cough drops and spit into the bathroom sink. In the dark there are wasted keystrokes as I hit the wrong square, hoping for an *n* but tapping an *m* instead. Despite the inconveniences, this is how books are finished, in the same margins we started in. The writer and coach Cynthia Morris calls it being an ardent opportunist—someone willing to see potential in all circumstances, from waiting rooms to nature walks.

I've written this book in a variety of places:

> My living room couch
> My living room chair, feet propped on an ottoman
> My dining table, using a document easel
> A coffee shop on my lunch break
> A library across the street
> JFK airport
> An airplane somewhere over the Sierra Nevada
> Hotel rooms
> The front seat of my car
> The back seat of my car
> A patio
> A parking lot
> A bench in the office building next door to mine
> My bed, with the noise of *Cars 3* playing softly in the background

Today I write in the dark, and it's providing an unforeseen gift. For a few sacred moments, I can slip into the quiet cocoon of my mind to write as honestly as I can.

In the absence of light, I'm limited to feeling my way through, like the time I found myself driving down a winding road in Michigan before sunrise, starting my journey home from a weekend book festival. The road was familiar. I'd navigated it the past few days, learning the curves, the length between turns, but never at this hour. When I first arrived, the event coordinator told me to look out for deer. "You'll see their eyes first. And if there's one, there's probably another," Bess said. Alone, gliding, I thought of the analogy by E. L. Doctorow, which reminds us that to write a book, we only need to see as far as our headlights. We're assured the entire trip can be made this way, the road half-lit. It never occurred to me the analogy might one day become literal, that I would grip a steering wheel at four in the morning, praying I wouldn't hit an animal on the way. Around the next curve an elegant head lifted, mouth full of dew-speckled grass. Her white-tipped ears flicked and she gazed at me. I quickly looked for another deer, but there was only one that morning. Bess was right about the eyes, which glistened even in darkness, as a lighthouse would, guiding me to the harbor.

Soon Henry will wake and call for one of us. We'll change his diaper and his shoes and drive to the beach before dinner. But for now, as brief as it lasts, there's nothing to do but listen, and type as many words as possible.

The Writing Project

To finish what we start, plans help. They're most useful when writing under a deadline (self-imposed or otherwise) because keeping yourself loosely on track, especially while juggling other obligations, is one of the best ways to build momentum. While I'm partial to strategies, I prefer them with softer edges. One day doesn't always have to be like the next. We need space to fine-tune, to step back, to reevaluate, plus generous helpings of kindness toward ourselves. A plan should honor the fact that every hour can feel different, yet there is still work to do. So I'll tell you how I set out to start and finish *Wild Words*, in case it's useful.

I've worked with many project managers in my career and have taken on the role myself on occasion. There have been annual reports, private dinners, new websites, and conferences planned start to finish, all with deadlines and timelines to uphold. I'm also married to someone whose job is to manage people and projects, so he's taught me many foundational practices. You might say the space of planning, organizing, making timelines, and getting things done is a sweet spot of mine, and as a writer these skills have benefited me more times than I can count. But like those soft edges I mentioned, these guidelines don't have to be a heavy, unforgiving boulder on your back. In the context of your writing life, project management can serve as a container to hold big dreams and keep you accountable to making progress, managing expectations, and finishing the work you start.

Have I always been a natural planner? Yes. I was the student who started researching her term paper the day it was assigned, and never once stayed up all night to write eight pages before class the next morning. When it came to writing my own poetry and short stories, I scoffed at deadlines and to-do lists, preferring to let inspiration strike when it chose, which in those days was often. It's easy to embrace inspiration in your twenties. (If you're currently in your twenties and reading this book, enjoy the decade!) But my life looks different now. I have a full-time job, a toddler, a marriage. And I want to keep writing books and blogging and encouraging people and all the rest of it. That's why when people ask me how I'm able to get it all done, my answer comes down to this: I make a plan.

There are a few things project management is ideal for. First, it helps you see the big picture. Writing a book or maintaining a blog involves long-term commitment, and to sustain it for any length of time, you need to take inventory of what the work entails. How else will you be able to bend it into the shape of your life? Once those details are clear, you work backward to figure out how much time you need to accomplish it. I remember a writer once told me her hope for the month was to write five thousand words, a number that utterly scared her to share publicly. But I did a little math and figured out all she needed to do was to write one hundred and sixty-six words a day for thirty days. Suddenly, it seemed a lot easier.

Another benefit is allocating your precious time wisely, putting it toward its highest use. Knowing what's essential and what's not enables you to sit down to write with confidence. (Revisit the essentialism exercise in The Season of Discontent for a refresher.) You aren't wasting time wondering what you should work on in a given week or month. This doesn't mean inspiration has no place here; it means you can maximize even the least amount of time you have to spare.

However, there's one thing project management can't always account for—creativity itself, cloaked in mystery, surprising us in unassuming moments while jogging or watering herbs. This great force hovers in the pulse of our bodies, propelling us onward, and is largely unexplainable with charts and templates. We might never know why writing is worth doing in the end, except that creating something from nothing always feels so right and good.

-Rituals & Routines-

PLAN YOUR PROJECT

Consuming endeavors, such as book writing and promotion, work-shop planning, or blog writing, warrant a bit of organization, and there are a few factors you can influence: the scope, the timeline, and the resources.

THE SCOPE. This phase is for determining what you want to accomplish and making big-picture estimates before breaking down all the individual tasks. You're guessing, you're dreaming, and you're not committing to anything just yet. Maybe you're planning to revitalize an old blog, or become a regular contributor to a website, or write a novella. Be sure to take your circumstances into account—family life, job responsibilities—anything that limits your time to write. Eventually you'll compare this to your timeline.

> In practice: I signed my contract for *Wild Words* the first week of December 2017, with a deadline of September 1, 2018, to deliver the manuscript. That gave me nine months to draft at least forty thousand words.

THE TIMELINE. This phase requires answers, or at least some strong guesses. How many hours does it take to publish a blog post?

How many poems do you need to write to fill a book? If your manuscript is due to the publisher in nine months, how many words do you need to write per day, or how many chapters per month, to keep the deadline? To gather some estimates, list the individual tasks you'll need to complete.

In my case, for instance, tasks included:

> Draft ten chapters
> Draft introduction
> Interviews?
> Research and reading
> Second draft
> Write epilogue—a trip to Malibu?
> Fact-check
> The reading-out-loud draft
> Find and replace commonly used words
> Early feedback from a few readers
> Final draft

With your list in hand, assign estimates, for example, two hours to draft an introduction, four hours to read a draft out loud, or one hour to write a blog post, whatever you think sounds right. (All of this will be tested and adjusted later on.) From here, write up a loose timeline to see where each activity can fit in a given week.

The bulk of your time will be spent straddling two types of writing: shallow and deep. It's the difference between dipping your hand into the translucent surface of water from the safety of a boat and sinking into its dark, murky depths while scuba diving at night. Writing in the margins is shallow work, and you've likely been doing a lot of it already. You know the trappings: taking notes, organizing a document, pondering a scene while you run errands, birthing the first draft. This is often done alongside distractions, with noise, in slivers of a day. Only now, moving into the third and final draft, am I shifting to the necessary deep work, which requires longer stretches of time where incomplete thoughts can become whole, sentences are polished, and revision is approached with ruthlessness. Deep work is the harder of the two, but it illuminates the path, making you feel like something might come of these words after all. Arriving at the shore of deep work is not an accident—it's something I prepare for.

> In practice: When I started my second draft, I thought it might take an hour per chapter to input all the edits from my printed pages. But when I got up from my dining room table one afternoon after an hour of work, I'd only rewritten five pages. So I took a look at my timeline, made some adjustments, and continued. A few weeks later I'd scheduled writing sessions in my calendar for Sunday afternoons, when I could focus on the deep writing needed to pull everything together.

THE RESOURCES. "Protect the team," Andrew often says. This advice applies to solo writers, too. When you have a lot going on, and specifically if you have a family or share your living space with someone, you have to ask for what you need. Maybe your mom can watch your kids for two hours each week. Maybe you need to decide whether you'll keep struggling to use Photoshop or take a course on it or outsource. Maybe you need to reflect on how much time is required, and what you can handle in the moment.

You might need:

> A social-media scheduler
> Photo software
> A host for your new blog
> An editor
> A cover designer
> Time to write
> Childcare
> A new computer case
> Extra computer memory

What I've needed:

> Time to write on the weekends
> All manner of technology: laptop, Google Docs, and apps
  for my phone
> Notebooks with a favorite pen
> Daily walks, five to ten minutes each
> Frequent yoga classes
> Places to escape: the beach, coffee shops, a writing retreat
> Mugs of tea

What comes next? Test your theories. Allow the first month or so to pass with curiosity as you gather information. Take care not to make any grand gestures toward your project; simply go about your days and fit in your writing when you can. Notice where those margins fall, where your energy peaks, and identify what you might give up to make space for the work you must do. You'll notice some patterns after a few weeks, and really firm up your estimates of how long it takes you to finish a task. Then you make changes and modify expectations, if needed. (They are almost always needed.)

And a word of caution: a well-managed writing project doesn't guarantee completion; discipline does. Showing up to write as many words as you can, as often as you can, finishes books. The plan might be a vessel, but it won't steer the ship.

Writing in Transition

After a week of unseasonal, 100°F heat, clouds arrived and rain thudded down all morning. My writing was utterly fragmented. A page open, five minutes here, ten minutes there. Out for a walk after lunch, I criticized myself for wasting time. I couldn't see how the messy document, about sixteen pages so far, could possibly fit together. I left notes all over it. *This doesn't belong. Maybe for another section. Is this right? Boring. Find a different metaphor.* I needed to stitch it, mold it, write more. I made dinner and helped tuck Henry in to bed, but in a rare choice, I didn't go to yoga that night. Instead, I opened my laptop and started writing. Slowly, the sentences came together and I gained some ground, able to see the chapter now, like surveying the view from atop a hill, all unfinished and unedited yet somehow whole. The evening reminded me of what the writer Alexandra Franzen says: the day isn't over yet. It's a reminder we only need to keep trusting, keep thinking, keep writing.

This is emotional work, make no mistake. Highs and lows are unpredictable and unnerving, and I've felt them more deeply this past year than ever before. But in moments when I come to the end of a paragraph and think, *Yes, that's right*, my body also reverberates with thrilling surges—you know the kind—that start from my heart and reach down my limbs. I'm simply too far to turn back. Behind me, I can see the path that's been forged, the one I wasn't sure I would ever find. Sometimes I just want to stand here, marveling at how far I've come, because I also think I'm afraid. I know it, actually. In the middle, or even here, close to the end but not quite finished, my words are still hidden from view, untouchable. There are no reviews, no critics, no other voices to contend with.

When I was in labor with Henry, I'd been sitting on an exercise ball for two hours, moaning through contractions that kept getting stronger. Andrew rubbed my lower back, but it no longer soothed me. I looked into his eyes and said that no, I couldn't possibly endure another contraction and wanted an epidural. But as I stood up, a deep urge to push overcame me. Unknowingly, I'd gone through transition, the period when I almost believed my body couldn't do it, when I desperately wanted labor to end, when letting out noises I'd never heard before was the only thing that felt right. Henry was born twenty minutes later. The Season of Finishing is a transition too. The final weeks of preparation and editing, of avoiding the page, even with a deadline approaching. Of telling a friend you're thrilled, and the same day wondering if you're deserving. Hitting *send*. Saying it's done. It's all part of the triumphant ending, and the story you'll tell when the memory of writing so intensely begins to fade.

How to See More Clearly

Now it's summer. After my annual eye exam I ordered a pair of glasses from Warby Parker, but my new pair needs an adjustment so I drive to the store on Abbot Kinney in Venice. While the technician warms the frames, he asks what I do, and because I've been practicing calling myself a writer in public, I tell him so. "Really?" he says. "That's great. I wrote a book about a year and a half ago, but haven't published it yet," he tells me. I pry, and he divulges more: he's too close to it. After the effort of writing and editing, time away was what he needed most. Knowing the story so intimately, he couldn't yet see what was missing. I tell him how smart this sounds. He rubs my lenses with a cloth, says he's feeling ready to start up again and take the next step. When I ask how he knows it's the right time, he answers simply, "I can see it more clearly now." I say good luck before turning and walking a block to my car, agreeing wholeheartedly about stepping back, placing the pages in a drawer (or saved in a digital file) for a week, a month, a year, if needed. Sometimes the separation is as brief as forcing yourself upright to walk around the block. Move your body, move your mind.

To know when it's finished, my inner compass usually points to this question: have I taken it as far as I can? If the answer is yes, then I'm certain I've done the hardest part, for now, and the pages are ready for more eyes—editors, a trusted reader, and my husband, on occasion. Having wrestled with the early drafts, two or three at least, shaping the toughest sections one at a time, I need an outsider to weigh in. So begins the process of pruning chapters even more closely to shape the book into what it will finally become.

A few more things I like to do toward the end: Read my work aloud. Alone in a quiet house, I print my latest draft, hold the warm pages close to my chest for a moment, then recite it all, hearing words meet the air. I notice where I stumble and make notes. During another round, I look for repetition. Ideally from the start you'll keep a list of favorite words, ones you lean on and use frequently. I always notice more when I read aloud and employ the find-and-replace feature on my digital copy to discover the offending words and view the grand total. Then I search for the problematic words one by one and make adjustments. In my first draft of *Eat This Poem*, I used the word *nudge* no less than twenty-three times, an oversight I was able to remedy before it was too late.

The book takes over the house like a living thing. An old journal, opened and flipped upside down on my nightstand. Stacks of printed chapters, held together with paper clips, sprawled on the hutch. My purple editing pen left on the desk. These past two weeks I haven't been keeping up with self-care rituals. With a deadline this close, exceptions are being made, and yoga, baths, and early bedtimes have been unattainable. In place of these activities, the body electric, soul elated, and even if there's a bit of apprehension or fear, gratitude outweighs it all. Chores were the first to go. Weekly deep cleaning is now the weekly wiping of counters. I'm fueled by popcorn tossed with extra virgin olive oil and nutritional yeast. Mugs of tea sit by the sink. I'm saving the chilled champagne for a few days from now. My body knows how close I am, and it urges me on somehow, gives me permission to ignore its needs.

Henry's come back for a hug, squealing and chasing the dog. I squeeze his body and kiss his head. "Goodnight, sleep tight, I'll see you in the morning," I say, then turn back to the screen. When this is all over, it'll feel like an exhale, like the hormones leaving my body after giving birth, limbs shaking. Until then, I sit in my chair and write. I thought about leaving the house again, like I did last weekend, but decide to stay. It's fitting to finish the last chapter the same way it started, in a Friday-night margin. The dryer hums, the dog laps water from her bowl. Henry negotiates a few more minutes of play time while Andrew dismantles his crib and turns it into a bed. There is no silence here, yet the words find a way.

On my lunch break a few weeks ago I walked to the next building over and sat in the courtyard to read. A few pages in, I noticed a crack in the cement and the thinnest, lone green stem pushing up. It was not among its kind, but the sunlight must have felt invitation enough to at least try. Isn't that why we're here? We write because we can't *not* write. But we also write for the promise of growth, of understanding something deep within us that we're always better off having excavated.

HONOR THE PATH YOU'VE TAKEN

Once you ticked all the boxes on the checklist—final edits, saving your file as a PDF, submitting it to your editor, making photo copies—and all the paperwork is out of sight, you may feel what Toni Morrison has called "a kind of melancholy," an unavoidable by-product of book writing and book finishing. It might propel you into another Season of Liminal Space, or self-doubt could decide now is a good time to make you unravel everything you've accomplished. Welcome these seasons and you'll see, you won't be there for long. Because you and I both know we're never truly finished. One story might be told, but there will be others.

For now, celebrate and commemorate.

> Make a reservation at your favorite restaurant
> Write down everything that was hard, and burn it
> Collect rocks and arrange them in a circle on the sand, step into the center and feel supported by the earth for a moment
> Invite friends over for dinner
> Write about these glorious days in your journal
> Go back to your body
> Reacclimate yourself to the world
> Bake a cake

What you choose doesn't matter so long as you take some time to honor the journey you've been on. As for me, my husband and I are driving to Sycamore Canyon in Malibu next week, to the coast that holds some of my earliest writing memories. I don't know what I'll find there, but I'm certain returning is the right thing to do. The last thing to do.

I imagine what looking up at those pale, windswept sand dunes might feel like, standing suspended in time for a moment, the hillside holding me yet again, a different body carved from a different life. But if there's one place to explore a piece of my childhood and lasso some final thoughts to the pages of my journal, the sea is calling. Final sentences will be written in front of the translucent water and calming waves, steadying my nerves, my heart, releasing all these wild words to the wind.

Epilogue
Searching for Sand

I.

A plume of gray fog hovers over the water as we drive down Pacific Coast Highway. Henry's at preschool, and Andrew and I both took a day off from work for this pilgrimage, to trace the origins of my writing life. It's Wednesday, when heavy commuter traffic heads into the city, but we glide past gas stations, surfers bobbing off the coast of Topanga Beach, families finding their parking spot for the day, unloading coolers. We continue past the pier, Point Dume, Zuma, El Matador, beyond all the beaches you would think to stop at in Malibu.

"Keep going," I say as the Sycamore Canyon campground comes into view. On the left, a cove where I played as a child. "It must be right up ahead, we used to walk there from the campsite." Around a curve the dunes reveal themselves, unchanged, formed by surges of onshore winds since the 1920s when the highway was built. I step out of the car and swing its heavy door shut. Spray from the waves below immediately mists my face like a greeting, and some sun has broken through now, bathing the mountain with shimmering light. The colors, the haze, looks like winter, but temperatures give the season away. Heat comes at me from behind, sweat forming in the small of my back.

Last week I read an article about a sand museum in Tottori, on the western coast of Japan. Bullet trains don't stop there, and the shores are quiet for most of the year, just miles of sand dunes bulging along the coast. Then the landscape changes. Artists from around the world gather to carve designs from the grains, working for two weeks, nine hours a day, on sculptures that remain on display for months in temporary, open-air structures. The city's mayor has called the sculptures' ephemeral nature part of the attraction. "All the forms will eventually disappear or degrade or collapse," he told a reporter, and finds virtue in treasuring the impermanence.

II.

We forge ahead and up. I traverse low bushes, run my hands through wild rye while my feet sink, thighs strain, lungs burn. Some other visitors are on their way down, leaving us alone. I sit for a few minutes among the grass. To be here now, high enough to take in the entirety of the coastline, inhaling the brine of seaweed mounded on the beach, listening to rocks split waves in two, the thunder of it. Some years ago I absorbed this landscape, and it has never left me.

In 1992 I wrote about how we lost track of one of our cars in the caravan and how I was surprised there was no plan to recover one another. I wrote about how we woke early to catch tadpoles and frogs before breakfast, made a fire, washed off the day in showers that cost a quarter for a few minutes of hot water. What I saw, what I smelled, tumbled out of me.

Andrew lingers below, framing shots with the camera. I'm nearly at the top now, among anonymous footprints of birds and humans. A lizard shoots through the bushes, alarmed. This sea is one of the original sources of inspiration for my writing life: fresh words and forced rhymes, laughable now, printed with conviction in my notebook.

> We're on our way to Sycamore Canyon.
> It will be a blast.
> Even though it's only a week,
> It will go by quite fast.
>
> We'll go to the beach
> and play in the sand.
> We'll bring our buckets and shovels
> and pretend we're a band.

A motorcycle rumbles past. Overhead, a pair of pelicans glides into the horizon. The waves look taller than our car, a black oval below. Is this what it's like to remember being born? To emerge with only my hungers, my set of cries? That was the first birth. Sitting here, it feels as though there was another, a decade later, when I wanted to write and started with simple sentences, conveying nothing really, mere facts: I was here. We ate food. We buried each other in wet sand. I woke up at dawn. It all began during a warm summer.

This second birth, our creative birth, unfolds after we've grown enough to be conscious of the writerly impulses, poised to find a pencil and slide it across the page as words careen through us. This is the root of our origin story, when we enter an intimate relationship with creativity, one we may spend our lifetime seeking to understand and harness. This is the journey. Braving the writer's path empowers us to truly know ourselves. Without the courage to keep walking—keep writing—part of us remains in the dark. And those unlit crevices are precisely where the lessons are, both for ourselves and for those who might benefit from our words.

I've been to mountains and deserts and landlocked places, though they're not landscapes my soul craves equally. But the sea? "I need the sea because it teaches me," says Pablo Neruda. The rhythm of waves, a never-ending score, is the undercurrent of my being. I have often wondered why writing was given to me, but I can't argue with the ocean's roar.

III.

It's almost noon. We lock our seatbelts and I make a reservation at Rose Cafe in Venice while Andrew drives. Fog returns. We inch past the Malibu Country Mart, Pepperdine University high on a grassy hill, and endure patches of traffic.

Back in town, we're shown to a table in the outdoor courtyard and settle in over burgers and salad, contemplating the season ahead and an upcoming trip to Disneyland to celebrate Henry's third birthday. People are beginning to ask if we'll settle here, buy a house, where he'll go to school, and we don't know the answers. We often talk about whether or not to leave this place. There's a possibility, months from now, I'll say goodbye to a region that has shaped me, creatively and otherwise. Sycamore Canyon will no longer be a morning drive away but a memory.

Before we left Malibu I found a smooth rock shaped like a flattened egg, gray with small holes, molded by water for who knows how many years. I reached down for it, tucked it into my palm as a token of the excursion. When we get home I'll place it next to another stone I found on Whidbey Island earlier this year. A new ritual, rock collecting? If anything, it helps me remember the places where I've stood, offers some proof that I was there at all.

Three days later I'm typing up more notes. This morning we attended a birthday party in Santa Monica for one of Henry's preschool friends, picked up lunch on the way home, and now I'm trying to write. I eat a piece of chocolate and drink a glass of water first, then draft a few paragraphs. When my computer dips below forty percent, I close it with a thud, feeling accomplished enough for the afternoon, then walk to the kitchen to chop tomatoes for tomorrow night's gazpacho. I core their flesh and wonder again, is this what it's like to be born? The question turns in my mind and I wipe my hands, rush to the computer. I cannot risk losing the next thought: What happened on the sand that day, with the light, was some kind of miracle—sun breaking through for a few minutes while we climbed, letting me see the water from that height, frothy and cerulean, and most of all, letting me see myself. Bathing that young girl in warmth, in hope, before closing the sky back up like a portal.

August 2018
Los Angeles

Acknowledgments

To my readers, thank you for allowing me the privilege of walking beside you on the journey. We're in this together, and *Wild Words* is for you. Lack of time is the main obstacle I hear from fellow writers, and I hope this book inspires you to make space so your stories can emerge. Andrew, I can't practice what I preach without your unwavering support. The life we've built so far, and my ability to write while also parent and work, is only made possible by your pushing me out of the house on occasion or taking Henry to the park while I edit. Even before I started writing, my agent at Stonesong, Leila Campoli, saw the vision. Turns out you were right all along—this is the book I needed to write. *Wild Words* has been shepherded by the most wonderful collaborators at Roost Books: Sara Bercholz, Jennifer Brown, KJ Grow, Claire Kelley, Emily Coughlin, and Jess Townsend. Thank you for helping this book take flight and believing in its message. To Jess Thomson, I appreciate your helping lead an inspiring retreat where a portion of this book was written and providing early feedback on a section I was nervous about sharing. Finally, I'm grateful to my parents for finding the old notebooks where some of my writing first appeared. And Henry, who once saw a copy of

Eat This Poem and said, "That's mommy's name on a book? I want my name on a book!" If writing is your calling too, then I hope you find courage in your voice many years earlier than I did.

References

Introduction

Braving the Wilderness: The Quest for True Belonging and the Courage to Stand Alone by Brené Brown

1. Beginning

Still Writing: The Perils and Pleasures of a Creative Life by Dani Shapiro

Rumors of Water: Thoughts on Creativity and Writing by L. L. Barkat

2. Self-Doubt

The War of Art: Winning the Inner Creative Battle by Steven Pressfield

"Outsmarting Our Primitive Response to Fear" by Kate Murphy, *New York Times*: https://www.nytimes.com/2017/10/26/well/live/fear-anxiety-therapy.html

Crossing the Unknown Sea: Work as a Pilgrimage of Identity by David Whyte

Big Magic: Creative Living Beyond Fear by Elizabeth Gilbert

3. Going Back in Time

At Home in the World by Joyce Maynard
I Know Why the Caged Bird Sings by Maya Angelou
The Complete Poems of D. H. Lawrence by D. H. Lawrence

4. Discontent

Brave Enough: A Mini Instruction Manual for the Soul by Cheryl
    Strayed
Essentialism: The Disciplined Pursuit of Less by Greg McKeown

5. Listening to Your Body

*Women's Bodies, Women's Wisdom: Creating Physical and Emotional
    Health and Healing* by Christiane Northrup
"Slow Blog Manifesto" by Todd Sieling: https://www.digital
    manifesto.net/manifestos/11/

6. Raising Young Children

Ursula K. Le Guin, 1989 interview with Terry Gross on *Fresh Air*:
    https://www.npr.org/2018/01/24/580222946/sci-fi-titan
    -le-guin-wanted-to-stand-up-and-be-counted-as-a-writer
    -with-kids
The Yellow House blog: http://casayellow.com/2014/01/22/a-cup
    -of-kindness-yet/#more-3243

7. Liminal Space

Desert Solitaire by Edward Abbey

"Seasons" on *The RobCast,* a podcast by Rob Bell: http://robbell
.podbean.com/e/episode-115-seasons/

"The Four Phases of Creation—Part Three: The Fertile Void" by
Kate Northrup: https://katenorthrup.com/four-phases
-creation-part-three-fertile-void/

Simple Matters: Living with Less and Ending Up with More by Erin
Boyle

Letters to a Young Poet by Rainer Maria Rilke

8. Visibility

*Present Over Perfect: Leaving Behind Frantic for a Simpler, More Soul-
ful Way of Living* by Shauna Niequist

The Complete Poetical Works of Henry Wadsworth Longfellow by
Henry Wadsworth Longfellow

9. Retreating

"Lessons in Stillness from One of the Quietest Places on Earth"
by Meghan O'Rourke, *New York Times*: https://www.nytimes
.com/2017/11/08/t-magazine/hoh-rain-forest-quietest-place
.html

The Power of Habit: Why We Do What We Do in Life and Business by
Charles Duhigg

"The Revolutionary," interview with Lin-Manual Miranda
by David Hochman, *Delta Sky Magazine*, November 2016:
https://view.imirus.com/209/document/12358/page/82
A Return to Love: Reflections on the Principles of "A Course in Miracles" by Marianne Williamson

10. Finishing

Writing Down the Bones: Freeing the Writer Within by Natalie Goldberg
"Your Creative Routine Will Fail You . . . But How to Recover"
on *Original Impulse*, a blog by Cynthia Morris: https://www
.originalimpulse.com/creative-routine-will-fail-recover/
Process: The Writing Lives of Great Authors by Sarah Stodola

Epilogue

"Japan's Sand Museum, a Home to Ephemeral Treasures"
by Motoko Rich, *New York Times*: https://www.nytimes
.com/2017/04/10/world/asia/japans-sand-museum-a-home
-to-ephemeral-treasures.html
On the Blue Shore of Silence: Poems of the Sea by Pablo Neruda

Index of Rituals & Routines

Use this page as a starting point whenever you're in need of a creative nudge. I've come to trust these foundational practices over the years, and I hope you'll make them your own.

The Season of Beginnings

The Season of Self-Doubt

The Season of Going Back in Time

The Season of Visibility

The Season of Retreating

The Season of Finishing

About the Author

Nicole Gulotta is the author of *Eat This Poem: A Literary Feast of Recipes Inspired by Poetry* and the founder of Wild Words, a community that helps writers embrace the season they're in. Born and raised in Southern California, she lives outside Raleigh, North Carolina, with her husband and son. For book resources, visit thewildwords.com.